P9-DVG-268

Robert Francis
Collected Poems

DISCARDED

17.50

Robert Francis
Collected Poems
1936–1976

PS
3511
R237
A6
1976

UNIVERSITY OF MASSACHUSETTS PRESS
Amherst 1976

EL CAMINO COLLEGE
LIBRARY

Copyright © 1936, 1938, 1943, 1944, 1945,
1946, 1947, 1948, 1949, 1950, 1953, 1954,
1955, 1956, 1959, 1960, 1961, 1962, 1964,
1965, 1967, 1968, 1969, 1970, 1971, 1972,
1973, 1974, 1976 by Robert Francis
All rights reserved
Library of Congress Catalog Card Number
76-8753
ISBN 0-87023-211-8
Printed in the United States of America
Designed by Mary Mendell
Cataloging in Publication data appears on the
last printed page of the book.

"Blue Cornucopia," "Delicate the Toad,"
"Gold," "The Mountain," and "Suspension"
first appeared in *The New-England Galaxy*
(Old Sturbridge Village, Inc.).

"Come Out into the Sun," "Here by the
Sea," and "Superior Vantage" first appeared
in *The New Yorker*.

Section five of this book is a republication of
The Orb Weaver, first published by Wesleyan
University Press in 1960.

Woodcuts by Wang Hui-Ming

W H-M

For him my birches
Snow-bent are bamboo
And I among them
An old Chinese poet
One of the Tang. Ah
He too would be a bird
Uncaged a boat untied.

Preface

Dear Reader (and every reader or potential reader is dear to a poet), before you proceed further may I say a word? The first poems you will encounter, if you do proceed, were published forty years ago and most of them written some years earlier. If they seem excessively quiet, know that they were written by a serious young man whose most constant pleasure was a silent dialogue he carried on with himself, a prolonged solitary brooding.

As he grew older, book by book, he grew bolder and livelier, as you can see for yourself. Indeed, as he grew older his poems grew younger until, toward the end of this collection, some poems are positively frisky.

It may amuse you to follow his constant coming out of himself, like a mantis in its successive moultings. Only in its final moult does the mantis achieve its wings, and here our analogy breaks down, for this poet, like all poets, does a little flying all along the way.

If you choose to follow him all the way, you can speed up the journey by reading one poem every ten pages or so. Or perhaps, better still, you might open the book at random, as during the Middle Ages Virgil used to be opened at random, and you may, just possibly, happen upon an oracle.

Contents

Preface

Valhalla and Other Poems

The Sound I Listened For

The Face against the Glass

The Orb Weaver

Come Out into the Sun

Like Ghosts of Eagles

New Poems

1936

Stand with Me Here

A *Broken View*

Newcomers on the hill have cut the trees
That broke their view. Now they have all the west
From north in an unbroken sweep to south.
Outdoors or out of windows looking westward
Anywhere there is the west, the view.
An afternoon ago we stood with them
And saw their view. Hills beyond hills shading
From green to blue and clouds from white to blue.
Open places of pasture on the hills
And sky among the clouds. It was enough
For anyone to love for all a lifetime.

Yet we were thinking (though we didn't say so
And wouldn't of course have said so ever to them
Or even wished to) how we loved a broken
View better, a view broken by trees,
Under and over and through the branches of trees.
A view that didn't give you everything
At once or anything too easily.
One that changed as you went from window to window
And changed again as you went from month to month,
Closing in in spring and opening
In fall.

What we felt was not regret.
We had no sighs for trees that were not there.
Trees grow again in time or others grow
To take their places, more slowly than a house
Is built, but still they grow. Young trees were growing
Among the stumps there even while we looked
Over their heads.
                Perhaps we had a view
Through time, like a view trembling through leaves, of a time
When not these newcomers but a child of theirs
Or a child of that child living on the hill,
Growing up with trees upon the hill
Might see as we had seen, loving both trees
And view, loving them more each for the other.

Identity

This human footprint stamped in the moist sand
Where the mountain trail crosses the mountain brook
Halts me as something hard to understand.
I look at it with half-incredulous look.

Can this step pointing up the other way
Be one that I made here when I passed by?
This step detached and old as yesterday—
Can it be mine, my step? Can it be I?

Cloud in Woodcut

Make a woodcut of a cloud.
Polish the wood. Point the knife.
But let your pointed knife be wise.
Let your wilful cloud retain
Evidence of woody grain.
Teach your knife to compromise.
Let your cloud be cloud—and wood.
Grained in the art let there be life.

Firewarden on Kearsage

Rock on the mountain
And on the rock a tower
Sprung like a steel stamen
From a granite flower
And on the tower a man.
Call him a seer.
His slow relentless eyes
Hour after lonely hour
Scan and still scan
Horizons of a hemisphere—
A sky notched compass-wise
Each windy point a peak
Each peak a rock—
Chocorua's curved beak,
Washington, Moosilauke.
Speak: from the west can any shock
Shake off this granite petal?
From the east can any power
Break rock or man or metal?

Hay Heaviness

"I love hay more than any other crop
But corn," she said as we stood in the hayfield
Heavy and sweet in sun and wind with clover,
Tall with timothy that stood there ready
To be loved and almost ready to be cut.
"Now is the time," she said, "when every year
I feel the hay begin to press in round me.
I feel it even when I am in the house,
Even through walls." We stood there, she with the weight
Of years of hay that she had helped to harvest,
I trying to feel the heaviness she felt.

5

Four Women

I

She who loves the earth and all that lives
From the earth has something of earth's roundness now,
The satisfying roundness of a fruit.
Standing by the stove she stirs a kettle
Full of summer, summer of late September,
The last tomatoes, cauliflowers, peppers.
She stirs and stirs and stirs, over her face
A flush and something deeper than a smile.

II

Saying No too many times too many
Years has done this to her. Now she says
No perpetually with her head
Like a customer impossible to please.
Nothing will do. The salesgirl shows her days
In June and in October. Madam, these
Are the best we have. She only shakes her head.

III

Growing old this lady has grown straight.
You see her straightness almost before you see
Herself—the compassion of her eyes, the humor
Understated on her lips. Her gown
Is black except an edge of white at the collar.
The bows of her spectacles are steel or silver.
The years have done to her all that the years
Could do. Straight, always you see her straight.

IV

Why does she sit rocking hour after hour
In the curtained room? Or if she must rock, why
Should she choose to rock over a creaking board?
Wait. She has not chosen the creaking board.
She does not hear the creaking. She has forgotten
She is rocking. Only a little, only
A little longer and her chair is still.

Lady of the Flowers

She is a lady who arranges flowers.
Often she writes of flowers writing to friends.
"I have just brought in an armful of fleur-de-lis,
Pale yellow, and put them in a great blue vase
Against an old Chinese embroidery."
Sometimes the paper that she writes upon
Is painted with a flower, a Chinese flower,
And all her words flit round the flower like bees.
Even the envelope has a flower or two
Quite by accident—her town, her street.

Bronze

Boy over water,
Boy waiting to plunge
Into still water
Among white clouds
That will shatter
Into bright foam—
I could wish you
Forever bronze
And the blue water
Never broken.

Rana

Buddha never sat so still
Nor any graven Buddha sits
In any far and windless land
So still as this frog on the stone,
Part of the stone he sits upon
Beside the spring. Bronze-of-rock,
Water-green, sun-jewelled
He comtemplates the All. No fly
Garrulous breaks his trance and dies.

Onion Fields

Far inland from the sea the onion fields
Flow as the sea flows level to the sky.
Something blue of the sea is in their green.
Something bright of the sun on little waves
Of water is in the ripple of their leaves.
Stand with me here awhile until the white
Kerchiefs of the weeding women are whitecaps
And the long red barns boats—until there are
Only boats and whitecaps and white clouds
And a blue-green sea off to the blue of sky.
Wind from the onion fields is welcomer
Than any sweetness. We stand and breathe as we stand
On a shore and breathe the saltness of the sea.

The Outgrown Garden

Weed will be flower, flower weed, and names forgotten.
Grass will grow uncut and blossom and bear seed.
Wind will scatter seed as it wills, nothing moving
The soil but rain and creatures living in the soil.

For us whose hands are empty day will be long enough
For watching drops of after-rain holding the sun
On blades of grass in sunglow. Summer will be long
Enough, but not for gardens, not for playing God.

Hay

All afternoon the hayricks have rolled by
With creaking wheels and the occasional swish
Of low tree-branches brushing against their sides.
The men up in the hay are silent. Sun
And the scent of hay and the swaying of the ricks
Have taken away all their desire for talking.
They have lost count of the loads already in.
They cannot count—they do not try to count
The loads to come. More hay lies cut and ready
To be loaded than even the longest afternoon
Can harvest.
              Silent as bronze and color of bronze
To the hips, the haymen ride to the barn in waves
Of hay—New England Neptunes, each with his trident.
Along the beaches of the sky the cloud-surf
Mounts, masses—cloud heaped on cloud. The earth
Is heaped with hay. If a forkful falls from the load,
Nobody notices it. There is plenty of hay.

June, and the sun still high at suppertime.
After supper will still be afternoon
With ricks, a few, returning to the field—
Some farmer who will not trust a fair sky
Overnight. And when the sun is down
And the highest cloud pales and the evening coolness
Creeps up from the lowlands bringing the evening
Scent of hay and the sound of a dog barking,
There still will be, far down the field, figures
Moving dimly under the goldening moon.
Tonight the moon will light the last load in.

Meeting

Our paths happened to cross in space and time
And so we met, he going north, I west.
What he saw of me and thought of me
Remains unwritten. I saw a black snake head
Out from a shell and mesozoic legs
And tail. We both stood still and stared as if
We both could afford a few minutes so spent.
He was some hundred million years behind.
Had there been any question of right of way
He had it by those hundred million years.
I was the upstart. But there was no question
Of right of way. He had his path, I mine.
I waited to see him start. At last he started.

The Hound

Life the hound
Equivocal
Comes at a bound
Either to rend me
Or to befriend me.
I cannot tell
The hound's intent
Till he has sprung
At my bare hand
With teeth or tongue.
Meanwhile I stand
And wait the event.

ld age without a wife has made a wife
f him. He cooks for one, sews on buttons,
nd on Monday mornings hangs out his wash.
fter supper he and his cat stroll out
o superintend the growing of the flowers—
carlet salvia, magenta coxcomb,
de by side in peace. So he gets along
alking to his cat or to himself.

it is hard to die before your time
ith strength still in your hands and knees, it is harder
o die by wearing out, to die by days.
nce I planned to climb the Rockies. Now
m here. I can't take the first flight of stairs.
is hard to be a baby twice and weep
t the memory of anything or nothing.

I

aughter is easier for him now than talking.
hree meals a day and a pipe after each meal.
hat's that? He doesn't hear what you are saying.
e forgets what he was saying. So he laughs
t whatever it was, and laughs again to think
e can't think what it was he's laughing at.

J

e died at eighty. Out in the fields that summer
e had picked a stalk of Queen Anne's Lace
nd held it up to see the blue sky through
or the first time. While he stood there looking
here were three whites over the field that morning:
is white head, the white flower, and a cloud.

Earthworm

My spading fork turning the earth turns
This fellow out—without touching him this time.
Robbed of all resistance to his progress
He squirms awhile in the too-easy air
Before an ancient and implicit purpose
Starts him traveling in one direction
Reaching out, contracting, reaching out,
Contracting—a clean and glistening earth-pink.
He has turned more earth than I have with my fork.
He has lifted more earth than all men have or will.
Breaking the earth in spring men break his body.
And it is broken in the beaks of birds.
He has become and will again become
The flying and singing of birds. Yet another spring
I shall find him working noiselessly in the earth.
When I am earth again he will be there.

Roots

Here might a man, childlike, unbind his boots,
Go with bared feet, and sometimes, pausing, stand
To feel with the foot's depth the years of mold
Through which the buried roots, the living roots
Climb down to levels more profoundly old—
Eons of rock, centuries of sand.

Here might the foot feel and the slowed mind feel
What the root feels in its deep wanderings.
For mind can probe the obstinate hidden boulder
With fibers tenuous yet tough as steel
And climbing down to levels deeper, older,
Search, reach, and drink perennial springs.

Monotone by a Cellar Hole

Little is known and yet how much is known
Of these dead men who wrote tersely in stone

　　　　·　　·　　·

The sun shines down on stone. It must have shone
No otherwise than this when it first shone.
Wind blows as lonely wind has always blown,
A monotone not quite a monotone.
The sweetfern and the hardhack here have grown
More than all other living things have grown.
Now in the sun and on the wind a droning
Sound—a bee that flies and now is flown.
Little we know, little is ever known.
Life is. Life withers, crumbles—even bone.
Even the hard and bare residual bone.
And even stone, even unliving stone.

　　　　·　　·　　·

I hoard these stony hours. They are my own.
I am not lonely though I sit alone
Where other men have sat, and come and gone.

Pitch Pine

The pitch pine is a plain-man tree
Rough with masculinity
Any seeing man can see.

Its needles are no tree-girl's dress.
It scorns all pretty-prettiness.
Better the ornament the less.

The land it loves is any land
With plenty of stone, plenty of sand.
For dainties it makes no demand.

Small tufts of needles here and there
Bristle from the bark like hair
On a man's knuckle, in his ear.

Prophet

With an appraising, practiced eye,
Smoking his pipe, he scans the sky.

The smoke goes up to join the fog.
The fog comes down to join his thought.
Resting one foot on an old log
He contemplates what God hath wrought.

Smoke blowing west, smoke veering south—
He takes his pipe out of his mouth
And weighs the claims of rain and drouth.

In all fair weather he smells rain
So doggedly I wonder whether
He does not inwardly complain
That foul days sometimes breed fair weather.

But under this inscrutable sky
What can a prophet prophesy?

Artist

He cuts each log in lengths exact
As truly as truth cuts a fact.

When he has sawed an honest pile
Of wood, he stops and chops awhile.

Each section is twice split in two
As truly as a fact is true.

Then having split all to be split,
He sets to work at stacking it.

No comb constructed by a bee
Is more a work of symmetry

Than is this woodstack whose strict grace
Is having each piece in its place.

Boy's November

I can see farther now,
Now that the leaves are few.
November strips the bough
And lets a boy look through.
The ground seems tall somehow.
The far-off world looks new.
Tell me, can the ground grow?
Or is it I that grew?

Fall

Leave the bars lying in the grass.
Let all wanderers freely pass
In to the pasture now.

Gone are the fawn-shy heifers, gone
The little calf almost a fawn,
And the black two-year cow.

Leave the bars lying where they are.
Let each black-triangled birch bar
Be white and triple warning:

One for all tender things that go,
One for the near and ultimate snow,
One for frost by morning.

If that first snow a frightened deer,
Swifter than snowfall, swift as fear,
May pass here flying, flying.

What if no fence could foil his speed?
Spare him the leap, spare him one need
Of leaping. Leave the bars lying.

Toward Winter

I who love the rain
Was glad to see it go.
Glad when it came again
That it would come as snow.

I grasped a tugging tree
To watch the cold west clear.
I saw all I could see
Weeping a windy tear.

February Snow

Far and near and high and low
The world is nothing now but snow.

It sweeps and swoops down slanting-wise
In flakes of February size.

White is where black used to be.
Every tree is a snowtree.

Up in the steeple the hands of the clock
Reached almost III before they stuck.

This is a world without a bell.
Sleepers in their beds sleep well.

They sigh and dream, maybe, and snore
While snow piles on the bedroom floor.

Everything drifts or lies undone.
There is no time. There is no sun.

Slow

I have been watching slow things the long afternoon,
The thickening pad of snow out on the windowsill
That grows so slowly we can never see it grow
Although we say we can. All that we know is that
It *has* grown and most probably *will* grow so long
As the snow falls. And that is quite enough to know.
Then it will go and that will be a slow thing too
Whether it goes in sun or rain, whether a wind
Is or is not blowing. It always has been so.
And what is slower than this short, gray afternoon?
Slower than the way the sun, almost snowed in,
Begins by being low and ends by being low
And never sets or so it seems? Such a slow sun.
Nor is there much to show for *my* long afternoon
Except perhaps that I've been growing I suppose.
Only the unremarkable growth that must be, though,
Which isn't much, Heaven knows, for anyone to show.

Before

The sea was blue, the sea was green
Before the sea was ever seen.

Surf muttered its liquid word
Before the surf was ever heard.

And waves made time against the shore
Before mind thought its first Before.

The Wall

And there were builders building a wall.
They said: Let it be wide and tall.
They said: Let it be eternal.
And one builder would wave and call
To another builder on the wall
While cranes hauled stones no men could haul.
Small they looked, those builders, small
As walking flies. They seemed to crawl
Like flies crawling along a wall.

Now only flies are there to crawl
Over the stones. There is no wall.
The highest stones were first to fall.
Stone after stone they fell till all
The builded stones had fallen—all.

The Celt

I heard a voice clang like a brass kettle clanging,
Voice of an Irish bricklayer haranguing
Some lesser bricklayers. His clapper-tongue
Jangled as when a bell is jarred not rung.
Only the tone—but I could understand
The bile and choler of his tragic land,
The Celtic turbulence, wrangling and war—
Things that had been mere history before.

By Night

After midnight I heard a scream.
I was awake. It was no dream.
But whether it was bird of prey
Or prey of bird I could not say.
I never heard that sound by day.

Question

Have you ever seen
The feet of a bird
Clenched and crooked?
The bony beak
That will not speak?
The eyes looking?
Do you know what they mean?
Have you thought of the word?

The Curse

Hell is a red barn on a hill
With another hill behind the barn
Of dung. The road is stones and dust
And in the road are harpy-hens,
A hound, bones of cattle, flies.

Suddenly on Sunday morning
Out of the dew and stillness, a voice
Out of the barn God-damning cows
At milking. Whoever passes shivers
In the sun and hurries on.

First Sister

This beldam any season would be old,
But she is oldest when the days turn cold.
And when chill rain turns into colder snow,
She grows as old as age can ever grow.
Something about the sky's despairing gray
Reminds her of her own despairing day.
Something about the earth's unyielding white
Shows up the barrenness of her bleak night.
And rasping gusts of snow-encumbered rage
Blow through the bitter blood of her old age.
Grasping a broom, her symbol of defiance,
Like wily witch defying stupid giants,
She hobbles to the outer door to kill
The baby snow that sleeps upon her sill.
Then spirited by an excess of hate
She keeps on sweeping till she hits the gate.
Cold and numb are her hands. Not so her wrath.
She turns about and—double-sweeps the path!
Her broom, though still susceptible to dust,
Feels for cold snow a hotter, deathless lust.
But there is snow no mere broom can remove,
Old snow. For that, hot ashes from the stove.
Such is her ire toward snow.
                                What words suffice
To tell her direful enmity toward ice?
Clutching her hatchet that has long served fire
She haggles out her window, higher, higher,
Hacking the icicles that scar the eaves,
Then cursing those her hatchet scars but leaves.

Oh, does she never dread, being so old,
She'll break her neck or catch her death of cold?
No, for she's sworn nine oaths she will not die
While there is ice on earth or snow in sky!

Second Sister

Bewitched by blackfrost, withered like a weed,
Old Adam's wife has long since gone to seed.
She who was once fair, plump, and opulent,
Now bends the way a blackened weed is bent.
Drab as a beechnut, shriveled like a berry,
Dry as a burr and sourer than chokecherry,
She dreams of that lush summer when she sinned,
Dreams and tries not to hear the wailing wind.
For though to human voices she's stone-deaf,
The wind howls in a superhuman clef.
The wind that soon (who knows?) may whisk her off
Either by the hair or by a hacking cough.

So like a lurking basilisk she sits
By her webbed window in long spells and fits
Of staring at the thing that used to be
Her flower garden (back a century).
Staring and feeling swiftly alternate
The gloat of glee, the pangs of prickly hate.
For frost, both white and black, has worked her will
Killing the weeds her hands had failed to kill.
Once she would wrench them screaming by the hair.
Now she can munch her gums and leave them there.
Leave them to rear their heads head-high and higher,
Safe from the shears, the scythe, the spade, the fire.
But not from frost, she cackles. There's the catch.
For instance, that rust-colored tansy patch,
Tansy to lay a thousand corpses out.
(Tansy, you know, keeps flies from buzzing about.)
And there's her frost-nipped catnip grown to trees,
Catnip to brew a billion bitter teas.
But *her* bile needs a brew far more compelling.
Besides, her black cat's lost the power of smelling.
What with the frost, the wind, and getting old
He caught a racking, running, rheumy cold.
His purr is only an asthmatic wheeze.
Nine times a night he starts from sleep to sneeze.
No wonder mice breed in the flour bin,
Breed and feed and ask the field mice in,
Feed and breed and no one there to tell,
For she can't hear a mouse and he can't smell.

Betimes she grins and gives a soundless cackle.
(Her only sound is when her dry bones crackle.)
Cackles to think the foolish frost is willing
To do for her he hates her moil of killing.
But quick the bloodlust turns to quaking fear.
The leaves! The leaves! The choking leaves are here!
Hoarfrost that cuts the weeds off at the knees
Unhinges these shrill harpies from the trees.
Hissing like hidden snakes just out of hatching,
Writhing and rearing and at the window snatching,
Making sly lunges, leaps, and flying catches,
And scratching, scratching with worm-greedy scratches—
The leaves! The leaves! Oh, how her thin blood itches
To burn the blighted, blasted, hell-bent witches.
Faster and faster the fouling frost-flock comes.
She stares and stares and stares, and grits her gums.
Too well she kens the curse upon her head:
LEAF MOULD WILL BURY YOU BEFORE
    YOU'RE DEAD.
OR IF YOU DIE, DIE AND BE DOUBLY CURSED.
THE FROST THAT FELLS THE LEAVES WILL
    FELL YOU FIRST!

Third Sister

Only the owl-eyed cat who softly prowls
On the black mountain, or the cat-eyed owls
That swoop soundless from twisted tree to tree
Have ever seen her or will ever see.
Only the fire of phosphorescent eyes
Can burn through her invisible disguise.
Only wings hushed with felt, feet meshed with fur,
Have flitted near or crept up close to her.
What monstrous, moonless evil is she brewing?
What is she blackly doing, doing, doing?
Only the owls dare answer, who-ing, who-ing.

But after cockcrow, after the last mist
Has lifted, twisted, died with a last twist,
Even the bat-eyed mole, even the bat
Mole-eyed, can see what she was moiling at.
Branches all snarled, boles gnarled like strange abortions,
Twigs tangled, twisted into tight contortions,
Roots that are rock-bound, rock-wrenched, rock-distorted,
Everything tortured, bent, perverted, thwarted—
Old apple trees! Gray on the mountain shoulder,
Gray and disheveled, grim as the granite boulder.
Old trees, old trees. Only her hate is older.

Does any ask, Who is the witch and why
Does she wrest only apple trees awry?
Ask rather who should twist them if not she
Whose self was twisted by an apple tree.
Ask why the serpent twisted when he spoke,
Twisting the subtle truth until it broke.
And if one must ask more, then let him ask
Why man's long toil, why woman's wrenching task.
Why his hands broke, breaking the barren rubble.
Why her too fertile womb bred only trouble.
Why their feet rooted and their backs bent double.

Of all the kinks of convoluted fate
Nothing is twistier than twisting hate.
Hate roils hot blood in labyrinthine veins.
Hate coils cold cockatrices in old brains.
Hate is the rheumatism in gnarled knuckles.
Hate is the twister when an old back buckles.
What swirls the moon about the whirling earth
Think you? What hurled the planets into birth?
And in that inconceivable beginning
When God spun all the stars, who set them spinning?
Who was it set the sun and moon to sinning?

White apple blossoms, see, bursting from buds,
Flooding the mountain with their mist-white floods.
Can she not blast them, damn them back, resist them?
Or if that fails her twisted fingers, twist them?
Is there no whirlwind? Shhhh! No insidious worm
To squirm in blossoms till the blossoms squirm?
Oh, for some tortile, tough, resisting metal.
Nor wind nor worm can twist a pliant petal.
Petals—soft, silken, with that flowery smell
She knew long, long ago, knew too, too well.
Fragrance of Eden, Eden. Fumes of hell!

Dirge

They are the dead who died of thirst
With water near, who never found
The cool, unfathomable well
Or the deep pool they thirsted for.
Who listening never caught the sound
Made by contented water flowing
Over green contented ground.
They died despairing and unknowing—
The unnecessary dead who fell
Almost beside the reservoir.
But there was no one there to tell
Of water to those men in thirst.
And now it is too late to tell.

Walls

A passerby might just as well be blind.
These walls are walls no passer sees behind.
Or wants or needs to want to see behind.
Let the walls hide what they are there to bind.
Out-of-sight they say is out-of-mind.
The walls are cruel and the walls are kind.

Dark Sonnets

I

A formless shadow from a far-off light.
Then in the sand the sound of moving feet—
And we have passed each other in the night
On any sandy, dark, deserted street.
Whether you turned your head trying to peer
At me, also a shadow and a sound,
I cannot tell. Or whether out of fear
You passed, then after passing looked around
How can I say, I who could only see
Against the night something a deeper black?
This, this is the one dark certainty:
There was no touch, no word, no turning back.
One certainty: the sound of moving feet
And shadows passing in a sandy street.

II

We are the lonely ones, the narrow-bedded.
Our last "good nights" are interchanged below.
Then up cold stairs alone—the odd, the unwedded.
What do we know of night? What do we know?
What do we know except that night is blindness,
That on a bed one sleeps, or lies awake,
That after too long waking sleep is kindness,
That for the unsleeping, day will sometime break?
Oh, we know more. We can tell you how wind sounded
On windy nights, and how the writhing rain
Hissed on the roof, mice gnawed, and something pounded
Over our head—or under the counterpane.
We are the lonely ones. When we are dead
We'll be well suited to a narrow bed.

Night Train

Across the dim frozen fields of night
Where is it going, where is it going?
No throb of wheels, no rush of light.
Only a whistle blowing, blowing.
Only a whistle blowing.

Something echoing through my brain,
Something timed between sleep and waking,
Murmurs, murmurs this may be the train
I must be sometime, somewhere taking,
I must be sometime taking.

While I Slept

While I slept, while I slept and the night grew colder
She would come to my room, stepping softly
And draw a blanket about my shoulder
While I slept.

While I slept, while I slept in the dark, still heat
She would come to my bedside, stepping coolly
And smooth the twisted, troubled sheet
While I slept.

Now she sleeps, sleeps under quiet rain
While nights grow warm or nights grow colder.
And I wake, and sleep, and wake again
While she sleeps.

He Mourned, but Not As Others Mourn

He mourned, but not as others mourn.
One death was not a cause for two.
All that was deadly was his scorn
For what grief does and does not do.

Now we must live a little less,
Dilute the joys our dead will miss—
Such grief he counted spinelessness.
Called it not grief but cowardice.

With lives his friends had to defer
He filled his own life to the brim.
For them he lived the livelier,
And they, the lovelier in him.

And all the days and all the years
Loved ones had loved but had not known
He fashioned into bright careers,
He made them blossom as his own.

. . .

We mourn, but not as he would mourn,
For he is dead. But does he rest?
No one can bear what he has borne.
No friend can shoulder his bequest.

Simple Death

It is a little thing to die.
A little thing it is to lie
Down on a common bed and die.
There need be no wide watchful sky
To watch one die, nor human eye.
No inauspicious bird need cry
At death, nor flying need it fly
Otherwise than birds fly
Whether or not some man will die.
No man about to die need try
To die or wonder how or why
Or say a prayer or say good-bye
Or even know that he will die.

This Quiet Thing

They draw the sheet above the head
Quietly. Nothing is said.

Draw the sheet and close the screen.
What was seen must not be seen.

Every move is made with care
Though the thoughts be far from there.

Hands that softly shut the door
Have done this quiet thing before.

Shelley

Each had her claim.
To each he gave consent:
To water, his liquid name,
His burning body to flame,
To earth the sediment
And the snatched heart, his fame
To the four winds. He went
As severally as he came—
Element to element.
Each had her claim.

Legend of Orient Point

He could have been a seagod on the sand—
Sprawling, seagray-bearded, clothed in black.
And sea-like he was neither old nor young.
You would say, He sleeps as boulders sleep.
But he was not sleeping. He rose and headed down
To the sea with white leaves fluttering in his hand
And there he flung them as he might have flung
Himself. You have seen a hurt child stand
Staring, staring before he thinks to weep.
So he stood watching his whitecaps go
Until the last had gone, then turned his back
Upon the sea, and slowly began to walk
Westward up the long shore of Paumanok.
How could he know, weeping, how could he know
The book had even then been born? The book
No surf could outroar and no sea could drown?

Diver

Diver go down
Down through the green
Inverted dawn
To the dark unseen
To the never day
The under night
Starless and steep
Deep beneath deep
Diver fall
And falling fight
Your weed-dense way
Until you crawl
Until you touch
Weird water land
And stand.

Diver come up
Up through the green
Into the light
The sun   the seen
But in the clutch
Of your dripping hand
Diver bring
Some uncouth thing
That we could swear
And would have sworn
Was never born
Or could ever be
Anywhere
Blaze on our sight
Make us see.

Hermit

Blue frosty stones for eyes.
Bright hairiness for clothing
Except the loins in leather
Burnished with sand and sun.
A voice distant and small
As from across a space.
And no man could tell whether
He worshipped God the One
Or whether stone or fire.
Those who saw his face
Knew not if to call
Him mad or foolish or wise.
He had forgotten fear.
His body knew no loathing.
Warm in his winter cave
He did not shrink from sharing
His body's warmth with serpents
Whose shell-smooth skin is dry,
Whose delicate tongues are fire-points,
Whose ways are subtlety.
And in the hermit's ear
Always the sound of wave,
Always the sound of sea.

Appearance and Disappearance

Sand, sea, sky—
I count an ancient three
Before my narrowing eye
Encounters something more,
A dark identity
Far down the devious shore.

A thing so far away,
This speck, this human form,
No watcher here might say
A child, a man, a woman.
I see the simple norm,
The undivisive human.

Slowly it moves on
Beside the moving sea.
I look, and it is gone.
Again all I descry
Is aboriginal three—
Sand, sea, sky.

Comet

The comet comes again.
Astronomer, tell when.

When ends its long eclipse?
Where meets the long ellipse?

Plot its explicit path
In geometric graph.

Trace its eccentric course
Through the curved universe.

Expound to us the law
By which we see again
The comet we first saw
As boys, now as old men.

Days

Nothing between this day and days you knew.
Nothing of intervening years for you
To see if you were here to see. Nothing
Of time. The petals of the apple blossoms
Drown in the deep grass as they always drown
In grass in May. Greenness overruns
The air, leaving room only for birds
To fly and birds to sing and wind and sun
And you riding a small boy on your shoulders
Pausing to see and point a bird, the same bird.
Nothing of years, of time. Nothing of change
Except in us. We are older now.
Too many days (you smile and understand?)
Too many days like this have made us old.

Clouds

Blight and disease will never reach cloud-high
To touch those perfect clouds with flaw or pain.
Though they appear and pass, clouds never die.
Or if they die the beautiful death of rain,
They are born beautiful and white again
In this same sky or in another sky.

Farther than bird-flight, nearer than nearest star,
They only seem to rest upon the hills.
Thanks to all they are not and all they are
We rest in them our minds, our moods, our wills.
Moving with them we move beyond all ills—
Far from the ailing earth, yet not too far.

Apple Gatherers

Old men gather apples from the ground.
Young men gather apples from the trees,
Climbing their pointed ladders round by round,
Reaching always for those apples past these.

The old men hardly look above the ground.
They stoop, they kneel in grass like men grown lowly.
They move with little sound or with no sound,
And they move slowly, the old men move slowly.

What wind and ripeness once have reaped they reap
A second time. They find all to be found.
Theirs are the bruised, the broken, the cider heap.
Old men gather apples from the ground.

Invitation

You who have meant to come, come now
With strangeness on the morning snow
Before the early morning plow
Makes half the snowy strangeness go.

You who have meant to come, come now
When only *your* footprints will show,
Before one overburdened bough
Spills snow above on snow below.

You who were meant to come, come now.
If you were meant to come, you'll know.

The Runners

Runners going up the hill
Together as a single runner
Up the hill under the elms.
This is the final stretch. The hill
Is home. Sun filters through the elms
And falls on faces and on thighs
That lift and fall, lift and fall.
Leaves fall and imperceptibly
The sun itself is falling. Sound
Of feet striking the earth, of feet
Against the sunburnt fallen leaves,
Of runners going up the hill.

Homeward

Sun that gives the world its color,
Turn me darker, deeper, duller.

Make the clouds white, and the foam.
Make me brown as fresh-turned loam.

Save whiteness for sky and sea.
Give the tan of earth to me.

Blend me to the hue of loam.
Turn me homeward, turn me home.

1938

Valhalla and Other Poems

The Two Uses

The eye is not more exquisitely designed
For seeing than it is for being loved.
The same lips curved to speak are curved to kiss.
Even the workaday and practical arm
Becomes all love for love's sake to the lover.

If this is nature's thrift, love thrives on it.
Love never asks the body different
Or ever wants it less ambiguous,
The eye being lovelier for what it sees,
The arm for all it does, the lips for speaking.

Before the Lover

Before the lover was the lover,
Hero hero, saint the saint
Or son of god was son of god

When only the little boy looked up
At the mother looking down at him,
And what he said to her to him.

Before the lover was the lover
Or son of god was son of god
When only the little boy looked up.

The Name of Gold

Reserve the name of gold for gold,
And having named the thing be done.
Be glad that nothing else is gold,
Not flower, leaf, fruit, moon or sun.

Let each be color to itself.
Or let whoever must compare
The thing he loves to something else,
Find something comparably fair.

Summer Sun

Our living is a little heat.
For this we house, we clothe, we eat.

In winter burn the tree, the coal.
In summer sun us body and soul.

Yet all the heat we have is one
Essentially, the summer sun.

Only the summer sun burns deep.
Only the summer sun will keep.

We live to learn new ways to hold
Summer sun through winter cold.

False Flowers

False Solomon's Seal? False Lily of the Valley?
Whoever heard of such a villainy—
To call an unsuspecting flower false
Merely because it isn't something else!
To be oneself, this is Original Sin
Whether we speak of flowers or of men.

Mountain Blueberries

These blueberries belong to birds
If they belong to anyone.
Who could have planted them but birds
Three thousand feet up toward the sun?

They live on sunshine, dust of granite,
A little rain, a little dew.
In shape a miniature moon or planet,
In color distant-mountain blue.

White-Throated Sparrow in Massachusetts

South in September, north in May,
A bird that is always on its way.
And what it always seems to say is
   Old Sam Peabody, Peabody, Peabody.

Hearing the song I overhear
The coming and going of the year.
Going or coming the song is clearly
   Old Sam (sometimes without the Peabody).

Breaking the Apple

He took the apple I had given him
In both his hands and broke it clean in two
By way of sharing half and half with me
And showing me a trick strong hands can do.

How neatly and directly it was done.
Here was a truth he never learned at school:
Bare hands are sometimes better than a knife;
The man may be superior to the tool.

39

The Gardener

I watch an old man working in his garden
Dealing life to plant and death to weed.
Of one he saves, of one destroys the seed.
He knows the weeds and not one will he pardon.
He bids the pea vines bloom and they obey.
He teaches them to climb. He tests a pod.
Much that another man might throw away
He saves, he forks it under for decay
To be another generation's need.
This is his work to do. This is his day.
He makes all birth and growth and death his deed.
Slowly he moves, but slow is not delay.
He has all time to work. I watch him plod.
Old man, old man, who told you you were God?

Sheep

From where I stand the sheep stand still
As stones against the stony hill.

The stones are gray
And so are they.

And both are weatherworn and round,
Leading the eye back to the ground.

Two mingled flocks—
The sheep, the rocks.

And still no sheep stirs from its place
Or lifts its Babylonian face.

The Wood Pewee

In the shade of a tree in the heat of afternoon
The wood pewee sings his portamento tune
That summer is over-ripe and autumn is soon.

He sings from a twig after flitting to catch a fly.
And whether he sings September or July
He sings of the end of summer and sings goodby.

Waif

If he was never quite at home in his body
And all the air he took into his lungs
He never took as if he owned it all,
And food could never fully nourish bone
And muscle, and if there was no other body
Whose touch could teach him how to be at home—
Do not suppose his life was too too sad.
More than most men he could half-inhabit
Some old tree, perhaps, or some new cloud.

The Stile

I walked a casual country mile.
I walked until I came to a stile
And climbed up and sat down a while.

The stile was not yet obsolete.
The top step served me for a seat.
The lower steps served for my feet.

Not far away some pigs were lazing.
Off to the east gray sheep were grazing.
Westward cows were standing gazing.

I faced one field and then the other.
I had no wish to go on further.
Even the going back was bother.

So I sat there on the fence.
Sitting still seemed common sense,
And any change, irrelevance.

Rain

Mrs. A gets up and shuts the windows
Upstairs, downstairs, going from room to room
Because it is raining in or might rain in.
Mr. B turns from his right to left.
C only sighs. D is a sound sleeper.

Waking alone from having slept alone,
Hearing the heavy pour of rain on trees,
Thinking of trees in rain, he leaves his bed
And house (the last man Z) and goes and stands
Naked among the trees in rain a tree.

Early Spring

Down the street an old man comes out
Wearing a long black overcoat
Buttoned tight around his throat.
He takes a step or two, then stops
To test the sun and look about
Before he ventures off his stoop.

Starlings and grackles overhead
Meeting in a mixed convention
Jaw as if to wake the dead.
Their overcoats are also black.
The old man pays them no attention.
He'll walk a little way, then back.

The Plodder

I was the one who used to go
And I was the one she used to see
Plodding to my work through snow.

The second time she noticed me
She must have known that I was poor.
The third time did she pity me?

And pity me a little more
(With Goodness there he goes again)
Each time she saw me pass the door?

I see myself as I must have been
To someone looking out at snow.
I see myself as she saw me then—

A plodder. There was little to show
How rich I was to be a poor fool.
Little to let the pitying know
How little I felt I was pitiful.

Enigma

Nothing Egypt did
In her dark pyramid
Remains forever hid.

The undeciphered land
Is here beside my hand—
This pyramid of sand.

Dwight

My neighbor Dwight at eighty-five
Is reassuringly alive.

The years have had hard work to age him
And eighty-five have failed to cage him.

Do not his spadingfork and spade
Deserve at least one more decade?

Yet when that goes, it would seem wrong
If Dwight himself should go along.

Without assurance from his hoe
Butterbeans might forget to grow.

And missing him in spring some year
Perennials might not appear.

Much would seem wrong that once was right
Under the dispensation of Dwight.

Two Women

November seemed to haunt the place.
The house was colorless as rain.
Two women standing face to face
Were polishing a windowpane.

One looked outdoors, the other in.
One had white hair, the other gray.
One saw herself as she had been,
The other saw the other way.

They moved white cloths against the glass.
The glass was all there was between.
They did not pause to watch me pass
Or let me see that I was seen.

The clouds above the house were white,
The trees were green, the sky was blue,
And birds in sky and trees were bright.
But that was all that summer could do.

Solitaire

He lit the lantern and the three oil lamps
And carried the largest into the livingroom
And drew the shades halfway, then went outdoors.
The daylight was just dim enough for lamps
To show. He walked a distance down the road,
Playing the passerby, before he turned
And saw his lighted windows as others saw them,
Though now he was the only one to see.

He walked on till he reached a curve in the road
And saw the windows vanish. Still he went on.
There was no other light except a house
Off on another road across a field.
The winter world was lithographed in grays.

At last he stopped, half turned, and listened, listened.
The only sound was the brook beside the road,
A sound that winter could only half subdue.
Was it his watching of the moving water,
Darkly against the ice, that started him
Himself to move, now in the same direction?

Back at the curve he found his windows again,
Brighter for darkness, brighter for being lost
And found. Having come home so many times
To darkness winter afternoons and nights,
For once he was coming home to windowlight.

The Fate of Elms

If they are doomed and all that can be done
Should fail, if they must die and disappear
And we must see them dying one by one,
Summer and fall and winter, year by year
Until there comes a summer so bereft
That over river, meadow, pasture height
No last and solitary elm is left
Lifting its leafy wings as if for flight—

Let us not make our grief for them too great
And say we wished that we had gone before,
Making the fate of elms too much our fate,
Seeing the always less and not the more.
Though elms may die, not everything must die:
Not their green memory against our sky.

Recognition

The man you are, the boy you were
Have sometimes been together here

Like elder brother and younger brother
Of whom we say How like each other.

The boy you were, the man you are
Though far apart seemed not so far,

Seemed like a son and father rather
Of whom we say Son favors his father.

But there are moments I have known
When just a word you spoke, the tone
Of the word—and boy and man were one.

Biography

Speak the truth
And say I am slow,
Slow to outgrow
A backward youth.

Slow to see,
Slow to believe,
Slow to achieve,
Slow to be.

Yet being slow
Has recompense:
The present tense.
Say that I grow.

Balance

The sky is blue, the field is green,
The hill is halfway in between.

Halfway both in space and hue,
Too blue for green, too green for blue.

Seen from the field the hill looms high.
Yet how much lower than the sky.

Bonfire on the Snow

One winter night I caught the glow
Of someone's bonfire on the snow.

It may have been but burning trash.
It may have only been a flash.

But while it burned not all the night
Could make the bonfire less than bright.

And all the snow that lay about
Was powerless to put it out.

All that I love, all that I know
Could be that bonfire on the snow.

Blue Winter

Winter uses all the blues there are.
One shade of blue for water, one for ice,
Another blue for shadows over snow.
The clear or cloudy sky uses blue twice—
Both different blues. And hills row after row
Are colored blue according to how far.
You know the bluejay's double-blue device
Shows best when there are no green leaves to show.
And Sirius is a winterbluegreen star.

Return

This little house shows the degrees
By which wood can return to trees.

Weather has stained the shingles dark
And indistinguishable from bark.

Lichen that long ago adjourned
Its lodging here has now returned.

And if you look in through the door
You see a sapling through the floor.

New England Mind

My mind matches this understated land.
Outdoors the pencilled tree, the wind-carved drift,
Indoors the constant fire, the careful thrift
Are facts that I accept and understand.

I have brought in red berries and green boughs—
Berries of black alder, boughs of pine.
They and the sunlight on them, both are mine.
I need no florist flowers in my house.

Having lived here the years that are my best,
I call it home. I am content to stay.
I have no bird's desire to fly away.
I envy neither north, east, south, nor west.

My outer world and inner make a pair.
But would the two be always of a kind?
Another latitude, another mind?
Or would I be New England anywhere?

Symbol

The winter apples have been picked, the garden turned.
Rain and wind have picked the maple leaves and gone.
The last of them now bank the house or have been burned.
None are left upon the trees or on the lawn.

Green and tall as ever it grew in spring the grass
Grows not too tall, will not be cut again this year.
Geraniums in bloom behind the windowglass
Are safe. Fall has fallen yet winter is not yet here.

How warm the late November sun although how wan.
The white house stands a symbol of fulfilment there,
Housing one old woman, a cat, and one old man
After abundance but before the earth is bare.

Valhalla

I

The October day that Leif was twelve years old
His father gave him an ax to be his own.
When the boy fitted his hand about the helve
And thanked his father for the gift that his smile
Told how much he had wanted, they may have noticed,
Father and mother, that the hickory wood
Matched his hair as well as hard and soft
May match, and that the grayness of the steel
Resembled something gray in his blue eyes.
If the mother thought of danger, she said nothing.
Danger she knew was never dulled with talking,
The danger that must be and is best to be.

Edith, said John, this boy is not a man,
Not for a few years yet, but he swings an ax
Like a man. He cuts the wood and not himself.
He ought to have an ax. Well, Leif, what first?

Running his thumb over the blade, Leif grinned.
The dragon.
                He means that old dead apple tree,
Laughed Eden who was two years wiser than Leif.
Your dragon!
                But it *is* a dragon, Eden.
You know it is. We saw its eyes and tail
And all its crawly legs, Johanna said.
You were the first to say it was a dragon.

But Eden only laughed at her little sister
Half her age. When *will* you grow up, Jan?

Then both girls ran from the house, for Leif had gone
With his ax to challenge the substance, not the name.

From the doorway John and Edith watched them run
In the wind that was running with them through the cornfield
Where pale-bright tassels and leaves of the cornshocks tossed—
Up through the pasture and orchard to where Leif stood
With gleaming ax and windy towselled hair

Beside his dragon.
                    They saw him point to the place
Where the girls must stand—Stand there—and the girls obey.
At this the two in the doorway looked at each other,
Seeing the so familiar certainties.
But even while he looked, her eyes grew dark
As water darkens under a sudden cloud,
The blue a different blue. If this was fear,
It had as little reason as a cloud,
And what it was a fear of had no name.

The distant sound of the ax made them look up
Again and see Leif's tossing shock of hair
And his arms and shoulders swinging rhythmically
And the gleam of steel. They listened as the wind
Carried the sound away or let it come,
Away or come, away—
                    Leif stopped, straightened,
Put both his hands against the tree and pushed.
It swayed, tilted, fell while the sisters screamed
Delight into the wind and danced about
The dragon all the more a dragon down.
Leif chopped the treetrunk clear of the stump, then turned
To see if they were watching from the house.
They waved to him congratulations, and John
Cupping both hands like a conchshell to his mouth
Blew three times Come.
                    The girls ran toward the house.
Leif, shouldering his ax, strode after them.

Another job for you and your ax, John said.
His words were less command than statement of fact.
His look was statement of fact hiding a question.

Fresh from one fight and ready for another
Leif walked beside his father toward the barn.

Now that you've killed a dragon, killing a hen
May strike you as a little commonplace.
But a living hen at least is more alive
Than any dragon.
                    They stopped by the chicken yard
Where a gray and whiskered man was scattering corn.

Sylvester, Leif is here with his new ax
To kill a hen. Will you tell him which to take?

Sylvester looked from John to Leif to John.
He knew Leif's unacknowledged fear of blood.
Having decided which hen was doomed to die,
He pointed her out to Leif. You want I'll catch her?

Leif will do the catching, John said. Leif,
Are you ready?
                    The boy unsmiling, almost untanned
Looked at the ground. I'd rather not.
                                        Not catch her?

No, kill her.
              Why not? John's eyes reached down in his
With a power to draw out what was hidden there.

A moment, then Leif said quietly, I'll do it.

Pale as if his blood were shrinking from blood,
He stole up to the hen as soft and quick
As death. But the way he held her with his hands,
Folding her wings together, smoothing her feathers—

You know the way, do you, Leif? His father asked.
I know the way, Leif said.
                              The squawking ceased
And the struggling. Holding the hen close to his face
Leif seemed to whisper something in her ear
At which her beady eyes blinked understanding.
Walking slowly toward the chopping block
He kept his right arm curved around her wings
And with his left hand grasped her legs. Stooping
He laid her on the block, holding the legs.
She flopped, then lay mysteriously still,
Her head drooped over the edge. Leif took his ax
In his right hand, gripping it by mid-helve.

Remember, Leif, kindness consists in striking
Once.
        Leif raised the ax and brought it cleanly
Down, then sprang back but not quickly enough

Or far enough to clear the spurting blood.
Seeing it on his hands and clothes, he swayed.
He looked at his father as if he did not know him,
But saw those eyes forbidding him to fall.
He could not look away from the eyes. He stood.

Well done, said John.
                    And old Sylvester's face
On which the boy's white struggle with himself
Had been reflected, now relaxed a little.
I couldn't have turned the trick better myself.

How many fowl do you suppose you've killed,
Sylvester? John asked. Not the pleasantest job
For you or anybody anytime.
He turned to Leif. We eat the food. We ought
To do the killing, our share of dirty work,
Though there was nothing dirty in what you did,
Not in the way you did it.
                        The hen lay still
At last. Her silly nerves acknowledged death.

Beside the house, flapping and leaping in wind,
The laundry danced and dazzled on the line.
The clothes were glad to be clean and dry and free
As any child could see. Sylvester's Ruth
Whose motherly arms had more than once held Leif
And Eden and Johanna all together
Was gathering in the clothes in two's and three's
As though she loved them.
                        Leif saw only the clothes,
The empty, flapping clothes. Within the hour
Something had happened to his make-believe.
They went in, Leif to wash and John to tell
Edith about another dragon conquered.

                    .   .   .

The high wind blew all morning over the hill
And afternoon, blowing loose leaves from boughs,
Then almost blowing them back. A few birds blew
From tree to tree, and one big crow blew off
The hill, using his wings only to steer.
The sun went down in wind though not a second

Sooner for it. A few things wind can't reach.

Within the house not one of all the twelve
White candles on the dining table fluttered
Except when someone passed.
                                          Eden came in
Bringing a loaf of bread that she had baked,
Bread dark with butternuts and hickories
Seasoned a year from old Valhalla trees.
But there was also something new in the loaf.
No tongue would tell till every tongue had tasted.
Eden smiled to herself as she set it down,
Warm and enticing.
                                Walking very slowly,
Solemnly intent on her task, Johanna
Was bringing in a brimming pitcher of milk
Warm from the generous udders of Audhumbla,
The white Ayrshire whose milk mothered them all.

Leif brought in logs of white birch for the fire
Suddenly brighter than all the twelve white candles.

When they sat down at last, Johanna stood
A moment longer to count them. Seven, she counted.
Seven for her just as the twelve for Leif.
They laughed gently at her interpretation,
All except Leif whose face in the moving light
Was half a smile and half a far-away-ness.

Lifting his glass, John said, Before we eat
Let's drink a health to Leif the Dragon-killer.
Next to our loyal friends and honored guests
This evening, Lady Ruth and Sir Sylvester.
And last a long health to our hill and home
And all we are and have and love—Valhalla.

As if the wind had been waiting for this pause,
It rushed at the windows and door in a fiercer effort
To force itself inside. But after that
They did not seem to hear it any more.
Johanna thought it must have given up
Or gone to try a house on another hill.

With a blade as bright as Leif's ax, John carved the fowl
That Leif had killed, releasing fragrances
That had been blooming and blending in the oven.

The wishbone went to Leif.
                                    What do you wish?
Hurry, demanded Eden.
                        Don't hurry him,
Said Edith. Eating takes time and so does wishing.

Seeing Sylvester taking a bite of bread,
There's something new in it, said Eden. Guess.

I never tasted better. (Then very gravely)
But it would take a woman's tongue to tell.

So Ruth and Edith and Johanna tasted
And guessed things possible and impossible
While the laughing men did more to the bread than taste.
Even when Eden hinted flavor of almond
The guesses still went wild.
                                    Why, apple seeds!
The inside of apple seeds, dozens of them!
They taste like almonds. Don't you taste? I do.

Whatever put the notion in your head,
Her father asked with something more than amusement,
Eden, of putting apple seeds in bread?
(As though she knew, as though there were any answer.)

Again he raised his knife to carve, but paused
Seeing that Leif had also paused in eating,
His eyes on something not in the room and not
On the hill at all, and not for others to see.

Well, Leif?
            Leif looked up.
                                    Isn't it time to wish?
Eden and you? Your wishbone not clean yet?

Leif grinned apologies and put the bone
Between his teeth and gnawed till nothing was left

Of it but bone, then held it out to Eden.
She took hold of her prong and closed her eyes
To wish and smiled and opened her eyes. All ready.

Although Leif tried to make his own prong break,
It was her prong that broke.
                              What did you wish for?

Tell us, tell us, Leif.
                    I didn't wish.

You didn't wish! Why not? But that's not fair.

I couldn't think of anything to wish for.

Oh, that spoils all the fun, said Eden dropping
Her smaller half to her plate.
                              Nothing to wish for?
John repeated searchingly.
                         And Edith,
It didn't have to be a great wish, Leif.
Just for the fun you might have made one up.

But Mother, why should I have to make-believe?
(His eyes were shadow in the candlelight.)
I wanted an ax and now I have an ax.

The innocent boy, breathed Ruth for only herself
To hear. He doesn't know what wishes are.

Though you have none for yourself or us, said John,
We have for you. Now for some golden pudding
If pumpkins ever made a pudding golden.
Audhumbla sends her birthday greetings to you
In cream. You wish some, Leif?
                              The others laughed,
And Leif looked both forgiven and forgiving.

When the time came, he stood and leaning forward
Blew all the candles out with one long breath.

II

One window had drawn Edith more than once
That morning to its view of many things—
Pasture and orchard and beyond the orchard
The remnants of a few red maple leaves,
And Leif still busy with his ax and dragon
Although it was no dragon to him now,
Only wood for burning, wood to be cut in lengths
And stored to season.
             So she stood watching him,
Wondering what thoughts were moving in his mind,
What story to be told some winter night
While his wood was burning.
             And while she stood and watched,
The moment was a drop of window-rain
That seems about to fall, yet does not fall.
Her life was a light thing floating on her breath.
She ceased to see or think, almost she ceased
To feel and only was.
             A little while,
But when she looked again, Leif was not there.
And then she saw him lying on the ground.

She ran from the house calling to John, calling
No to the voices pounding in her ears
That it had happened, it had, it had, it had.
The maple leaves were blood on tree and ground
And blood on Leif she saw before she saw
There was no blood, but only Leif on the ground,
Pressing his hand against his side, and John
Lifting him up before he spared breath to cry,

Have Sylvester harness horse to take us to doctor's.
If it's appendicitis—
             He didn't finish.
He tried to run himself and not to run
Because of Leif's pain. He tried to take the pain
Himself and cursed himself because he couldn't.

Leif murmured only once a question, Father?

The answer was a steadying of the arms.
Let anything that might be looking down
Make no mistake: this was a child. If pain
Were coming worse—
                    They reached the barn and the carriage.
They got in, John with Leif, the others helping.
Edith ran for the blanket to wrap around him.
The two girls stood together, back a distance,
Awed by the sight of Leif in his father's arms
Like a baby, Leif not speaking, not even smiling
Except when his mother's smile of love and good-bye
Brought just a faint reflection to his face.
Nobody said good-bye. What would it mean,
Saying good-bye? Johanna slipped her hand
Into Eden's. Sylvester took his seat and the reins
And started. He kept the horse to a steady trot
Along the wheeltracks through the open pasture,
Into the woods, and they were gone.
                                        Faintly
The whistle of a train—the farthest sound
They ever heard except thunder. They were alone,
Two women and two girls, upon the hill.

Johanna drew her hand from Eden's. Mother?

But Edith did not look away from the woods
Where the road went in.
                        (Softly) What is it, Mother?

The window,—I was standing there, she said
Less to the girls than to the evergreens
Or to the clouds over the evergreens.
I was standing by the window watching—
                                        Again
The whistle of the train, but fainter, fainter.

Come, said Edith, we have work to do,
Both ours and theirs as well, as well as we can.

So they went in. Each found something to do
To try to make believe the house was the same.
They did the familiar things. Were not four people
Enough to keep a house inhabited?

To keep the doors from waiting, windows from staring,
The walls too silent and the clock too loud?

They ate like Sisters listening to silence,
Saying little. The meal was ritual.
Nuns never were aware of God as these
At table were aware of those not there.
Sometimes a name, as Father, Leif, Sylvester.

Outdoors the hill was stranger than the house.
You saw a cloud. Looking again you saw
That it was gone or double or different.
Birds for no reason flew from tree to tree,
And noisy flies spared by the first hard frosts
For the last warm days, buzzed ominously.
                                        The chickens
When they were fed peered up suspiciously
And shook their combs and talked among themselves.
Audhumbla let it be known something was wrong
At milking by the way she craned her neck
Around to see who else it was and why.
There was an injured expression in her eyes,
A protest at all change.
                          High overhead
A hawk lay on the thin air looking down.

Late in the afternoon Edith had paused
A moment by a window. She stood there seeing
Nothing beyond a familiar bit of wood
And sky—until she was aware of blood
On trees and on the ground, and of herself
About to fall. She grasped the windowframe,
Clung to it, closed her eyes, and did not fall.

Night was early, moving among dark trees,
Trailing their shadows down across the farm
Till all was shadow. A night that could bring rain.
They made themselves a lighthouse with lamps in windows
For any who might be coming up the hill.
Lamps had another unacknowledged purpose:
To keep the rooms of a house from being empty.

They sat together, the four of them, and waited
Although the waiting was disguised as work.
Johanna had heard her mother saying something
About her going to bed, too sleepy though
To start or to protest. In another moment
After another stitch or two with her needle
Edith would say, Johanna, don't you think—

But she didn't say it or take the second stitch.
A sound outside—and they were at the door.
Sylvester was alone on the carriage seat,
His face in the lantern light both grave and cheerful
Like an old-fashioned god.
                              The boy's all right.
I waited in the village till Doctor got back.
He'd waited till the boy was out of ether.
A bad case, Doctor said, but a good surgeon.

He's safe, Sylvester? He's out of danger now?

He's weak of course. They're feeding him warm water.
A teaspoon at a time. But he's clean of poison.
Appendix broke. They had to wipe him out.
The Doctor said they did a job to be proud of.

What was the time?
                              Round noon it must have been.
And John?
              With Leif, and will be for a day
Or so.
          Sylvester started down from the seat
While Edith held her hand to him, for him
And for herself. She drew the old man toward her
To kiss his face halo'd in lantern light.
Saying no word she left him and went to the doorway,
Eden and Johanna following,
Then hesitated, turned, and spoke, Sylvester?
When you are ready you will find some supper
Ruth has been keeping warm for you, Sylvester.
Good night and a good sleep.
                              Reluctantly
And late, the scattered drops at first, then pause,
More drops, and then the delicate noise of rain

60

On leaves on trees, and roofs, and leaves on ground,
Bringing another day.
                    On the third day John
Was home and almost Leif was back with him
With all his news of Leif, Leif eating again,
Leif smiling, talking, sending messages.

Ruth cleaned his room and made his bed up fresh
And moved it near the window. At tabletime
The food they ate was not so interesting
As food that Leif would have. When Leif comes back—
Eden was pondering how her recipe,
Leif's birthday bread, could be improved upon.
There were kitchen consultations every day.
Without consulting, John took down his shotgun,
Cleaned and oiled it.

                    .   .   .

                    If any line could be drawn
Across the year and separating warm
From cold, summer-fall from winter-fall,
That line was passed. The last red leaves had fallen.
Sylvester and Ruth had closed their house in the village.
Until the days were warm and long again
They wouldn't be driving down the hill at evening
And up the hill in early morning to work
As they had done so many times all summer,
Keeping their village life with their old house.
They were on the hill to stay, ready for winter.

Late afternoon with the threat or promise of snow.
The air so still that one would hear the fall
Of flakes when they came. And then the sound of voices
And John and a stranger with a pole between them
Slung from shoulder to shoulder and from the pole
Hanging by feet bound by a rope a deer.
The limp ears drooped, the head dragged on the ground,
And blood was on the throat. Johanna saw
And ran from seeing and hid in the dark hall closet
And closed the door.

                    Eden had darted out
Where the others were and the deer lay on the ground,

A doe. Its dark eyes stared as if they knew,
They understood but could not move to answer.
It lay there waiting.
                    Eden looked from the deer
To the stranger who had killed the deer (her father
Had only helped him carry it down through the woods)
Until some unexplained necessity
Had linked the two, the killer and the killed.
He was not a man, yet older than a boy,
And everything about him was dark, his hair,
His skin, his eyes, and the old slouch hat he wore.

Sylvester asked, You want to hang her here
In the barn? And John passed on the question, Do you?
Seeing him hesitate and guessing why
John said, Or if you'd rather take her home
We'll give you a lift. You live in the village, don't you?
And did you tell me your name?
                              My name is Judd.

Wasn't that your mother's maiden name? Ruth asked.
I knew her, and I knew your father too.

My father's dead.
                 He looked down at the deer.

Shall we go now, John asked, or after supper?

Why doesn't Judd have supper with us here?
Asked Edith. We have a place already set.
We'd like to have you.
                      He didn't answer at first.
Hunger was debating with distrust.
But hunger won. I'll stay, he said. And thanks.

When they sat down at table, Johanna was there.
She slipped into her chair beside her sister
And no one thought to ask where she had been.

What do you do, Judd, down below? John asked.
Are you a farmer?
                 No, I'm still in school.
High school, my last year, though.

                                He looked from John
To Edith. Something in her glance held his
Till he was telling her more about himself
Than he had planned.
                        After I've finished school
I'm going into printing. I have a press.
Would you like to see a sample of my work?

He reached in an inner pocket for a leaflet
That kept like clothing the imprint of his body,
And handed it to John as evidence.

While John was reading Edith also read
From his expression that he found it good.
And then she saw that he was thinking of Leif,
Of a time when Leif would also say, Next year—

Fine work for any man. How old are you, Judd?

I'm seventeen just going on to eighteen.

John repeated softly, Seventeen.

Then Edith, I think I never felt before
The fascination of printing, the clean white page,
The clear black letters.
                        It's dirty work, said Judd.

But so is farming dirty work, said Edith.
What real work isn't?
                        Eden glanced from her plate
And saw Judd's eyes intent upon her mother.
Johanna who had been watching all the time
Spoke suddenly, You're sitting in Leif's place.

His glance was startled as if a flower had spoken.
He searched for something beyond the simple statement.
But there was only a statement, a child's, a flower's.

Leif is her brother, John explained. He's twelve.
That makes him just midway between you two.
He'll soon be home now. You and he could be friends.

Supper was over and Sylvester waiting.
Judd said good-bye. The three men went outdoors.
They did not see Johanna following them.
At the barn she stood at the edge of lantern light
In the shadow like a creature from the woods
Whose eyes are drawn to a light yet held off by it.
She watched them harness the horse and lead him out.
But when they lifted something into the wagon,
She drew back from the light.

                        When they had gone
And there was only her father left and darkness,
She found her hand in his.

                       Leif will be coming,
Won't he, before the snow?

                      Before the deep snow,
Winter snow.

            And when does winter begin?

According to the journey of the earth
Around the sun, not for another month.
(Then as they reached the door, still hand in hand)
But we are ready, aren't we, when it comes,
Johanna, you and Leif and all of us?

The old year that had traveled day by day
Toward winter had grown tired and stopped to rest.
Turning to look at summer down the trail
And feeling sleepy, he sank down in the grass
And fell asleep.

            Out by the pasture elm
Johanna might have gone to sleep herself.
It was so strangely warm and still. No wind,
No birds, and all the insects silent at last.
She might have slept, but there were hills to watch
And all her thoughts to think. She sat so still
There almost seemed to float above her head
An atmosphere of thoughts, like sunlit air,
That morning she had sat by this same tree
And watched the valley road to see him come.
She had seen car after car crawl into sight
Along the ribbon of road and out of sight
As one of them she knew was bringing Leif.
Now he was home, and she had run from him.

He was sitting up in bed among white pillows.
White himself, though his eyes were darker, larger,
Having seen things that hers could never see,
Those things too far, too strange, to share with her.

Late in the afternoon she tiptoed in
And found him lying back among his pillows
Studying patiently the smooth white ceiling.
Quiet as a ghost Johanna stood
And studied him, till something (though no sound)
Made him look down and see her through the doorway.
Neither spoke or smiled. His glance was detached.
She might have been a picture on the wall
Painted to show how the eyes of a little girl
May hold both love and fear.
                                    Do you want your ax, Leif?

Gradually his lips curved to a yes.

When she returned, his arms were reaching out.
I have been keeping it safe. I brought it in.
They would have left if lying in all the rain.

His hand moved lovingly along the helve.

Suddenly the room became too small
For happiness. Johanna slipped outdoors.

Off to the east the elm hung in the haze—
A tall vase without its leaf bouquet.
Or was it a bird, a great blue heron poised
On stilted legs, lifting its droopy wings?
A vase or bird or Lady of the Elm
With wide-sleeved arms outspread to feel the wind
If there had been a wind. So many times
Johanna had watched that lady standing there.

And then the elm became a ship with masts.
Snow would be sails. And all the hills were waves.
                    .   .   .
One morning Doctor Moor sat by Leif's bed
To say hello and tell him his wound was healed.
He had jerked away the last adhesive tape

While Leif's eyes on the doctor's had not winced.
The doctor felt about the scar with his fingers,
Smiling his approval, then laid his hand
Against the boy's bare belly to see how *that* was.
He laughed and Leif laughed back against his hand.

No chopping trees down for a month or two
Or three, he said to Leif and John and Edith.
The boy will be as good as new as soon
As that side is strong again. As good as new.
That means (turning to Leif) as good as a baby,
The good baby you were twelve years ago.

He started from the room, John following.
My job is done. If I were merely a doctor,
Or let us say, If I were more of a doctor,
I should have nothing more to say. As it is,
I do have something more, if you will hear it.
Have you a minute?
                    I have time to hear
Whatever you have time to say. Sit down.
I'll close the door.
                    First my congratulations
Upon your excellent luck. Do you object
To being lucky, to being known to be lucky?
It's luck we have a surgeon in Vermont
As good as any other in New England.
Luck that we found him home when we needed him.
Maybe a touch of luck that I was home
Myself, mere country doctor that I am,
A certain pleasant morning in October.
It was pure luck the morning was October,
Not January with the hill in snow.

I call it luck too.
                    What I should like to ask
Is this: are you not leaning on your luck
A little too securely, a little too
Serenely? Judging by the luck of others,
Their lack of it, you may be needing me
Again sometime that may not be October.
Wouldn't say half the year be almost as good
Or better than the whole year on your hill?

Being alive at all is dangerous,
Said John. You know that axiom better than I.
Bones are broken at every altitude.
And people die in cities every day.
One can hide from danger and think that he is safe,
Or one can live a life that's worth the danger
That's bound to be.
                    I like the sound of that.
God, but I wish more men were men to say it.
You, your family are the cream of the earth.
You are and have the cream of everything.
And yet we cannot live on cream. I mean,
We need all kinds of people, skim-milk people
As well as others. Would you be what you are
If many people had not made you so?
Where are the people that will make your children?

John looked away from the doctor's face to something
Beyond a window, on another hill.
That is a problem. Problems are to be solved.

But how will you solve it? Haven't you run away
From a solution? People are dangerous,
I grant you, full of germs, neuroses, lusts.
Yet people are not so dangerous after all
As none.
            John smiled a little bitterly.
I understand there are two counts against me.
First, I expose my children to needless danger.
Second, I shield them from desirable danger.
Perhaps I should plead guilty to both counts.
But Doctor Moor, to your charge of running away
I plead not guilty.
                    Did I say Run away?
You run away? If there is anything
You've missed, it is not because you ever ran
From it or ever thought or dreamed of running.
You may—I suppose that on a hill one might—
You may have overlooked one thing or another.
It would be easy. Tell me, when Leif grows up,
What girls will there be for him to fall in love with?
And Eden, what boy has she to dream about
In a year or two or now?

John did not answer.
Both men knew that they had reached a draw.

The doctor went to Leif's door, poked in his head,
Called Merry Christmas, because, as he explained
The next time he was there it might be time
For Happy Easter.
                    Dr. Moor, said John,
Thank you for being all you are to us.

                    .   .   .

Again twelve candles burning at suppertime,
Leif's birthday over again, Johanna said.
And so it seemed. The same seven at table,
With Ruth looking across the candles at Leif
To see if there were any visible thing
To tell Leif now from Leif two months before
Dreamy and distant in the candlelight.

What, venison? he cried. Who shot the deer?

Johanna started to speak, then waited for Eden.
But Eden let her father tell the story,
The shooting of the deer, and now this gift.

When he had finished and all were silent a moment,
Edith smiling whispered, Do you hear it?

Hear what, Mother?
                    Listen.
                              Then one answered
And all the others echoed softly, Snow.

The infinitesimal tinkle of fine flakes
In little gusts brushing against cold glass.
And blurs of whiteness flurrying out of the black.

Tomorrow, Sylvester said, we'll see some snow.

They looked at one another as if to learn
What it might mean to them. The candles paused.

Leif glanced at Johanna, found her watching him.

The dark boy sat in your chair at supper, Leif.

III

If any snow was left at all on the hill,
It was hidden in some deer-and-hemlock hollow.
Windflowers and rue anemones were white
In the open woods and in the pasture bluets,
Less blue than white, grew with the first green grass.

And Leif was racing barefoot over the pasture
Out to Audhumbla and the farther hills,
Leaping and calling to Eden and Johanna
Running after, and after them to Edith
And John walking, John playing his flute.
The tune was a running hornpipe, but the children
Outran the music.
                    Hearing their serenade
Audhumbla turned toward them with an expression
Surprised, amused, resigned, bewildered, sad.
Whatever they thought of, there it was in her eyes.
Then having looked at them, she turned away
Deliberately and would not look again.
They laughed and Eden garlanded her arms
Around Audhumbla's neck and laid her cheek
Against the cow's soft ear to comfort her
For being cow and to let her know their love.

A slow and triple tune, a sarabande
The old world would have called it. In the new
It had no name. Edith was barefoot now
With the children, and they began to dance a dance
That she had taught them in other springs, she
Herself untaught, unless the moving of clouds
Across the sky and the swaying of tall grasses
And long watching them had been her teachers.

So they moved measuredly, now grave, now smiling,
Making a quiet pattern of their feet

Against the ground, sometimes lifting their arms
To make another pattern in the air—
The two girls, Edith in the center, Leif.

Pausing for breath, John handed the flute to Leif
Who tried the keys with his fingers and shaped his lips
To play (for he had learned to play a little).
And three of them danced as they had done, until
One note went wrong, and Leif, darting his head
Downward as if to catch the faulting note
Faulted the next. Eden's delighted laugh
Tumbled the tune to the ground together with Leif
Where he lay on his back, kicking heels overhead
And making the poor flute squawk in agony.

Eden acted it out in pantomime.

Johanna, disapproving but forgiving,
Waited.
          Only Edith kept on dancing,
Smiling as if she still could hear the music,
Undisturbed until the dance was done.

Ruth had been watching from the house. They waved.

They're going down the hill tonight, said Eden,
And sleep at home. I'd love to live in the village.
Neighbors passing by all day, and at night
Their windows blossoming like buttercups.

But wouldn't the stars be farther off down there?
Johanna said. They wouldn't be as bright.

Beneath them and beyond, the valley lay,
The houses whiter for sunshine, and the road
That lost itself in trees and found itself
So many times, and on the road one horse
And cart that almost didn't move at all.

When the time came for appleblossom petals
To ripen and the wind to come and pick them,
Eden's peas were nearly ready to bloom.

Eden had been helping them with her hoe,
Keeping the earth dark round their dark blue-green.

Mention of peas could make the others smile.
What are you going to plant in your garden, Eden?
Peas, she had said, as if peas would be all,
Then added as an afterthought, And sweetpeas.

Peas and sweetpeas, her father had repeated
In a tone that made even Eden laugh. Why peas?

Because I want my garden early, she said.

So Eden's garden was called a garden of peas.
Peas took precedence over all other seeds.
They were large enough to be put in one by one.
Kneeling, Eden bent so close to the ground
Her sunlight hair drooped down and nearly touched.
She might have been planting thoughts instead of seeds,
Or thoughts with seeds, for every seed a thought,
The two to grow together in the ground.

While hoeing, Eden happened to look up
In time to see the wind walk through the orchard
Picking petals. Would any of them be left
The wind by the time the first peablossom bloomed?
Did the blossoming of peas and apples over-
Lap? And when the last peablossom fell,
What would be blooming then? So flower by flower
She dreamed ahead until she found herself
In summer.
                    It was a morning in July
When the men were getting in the last of the hay
That Doctor Moor drove up Valhalla hill.
He saw the rick and the three off in the mowing
And started out on foot across the field.
They did not see him coming or see him stand
A while to watch them a dozen rods away.

The rick was two-thirds loaded, Sylvester on top,
His wide straw hat the color of hay, his shirt
Only a shade a deeper blue than sky.

Leif cocked the windrows for his father to lift
And carry Atlas-like above his head.
Hay caught in his hair or trickled down his shoulders.
The brown of body made the hair appear
Albino, John and Leif the same.
                                        Hello,
Called Doctor Moor as he hurried off his coat
Before they could invite him to and laugh.
Leif, my boy (he was rolling up his sleeves)
I want to borrow your fork for a little while.

Leif handed it to him and stood aside
To watch, smiling appreciatively.

John and Sylvester did not slacken their pace.
They kept on steadily as if to say
This was their work and not to be deferred.
Scarcely a word while the three men worked together
Until Sylvester called down, Hold it, hold it.
John ran his fork into the solid load,
Then held his hand out to the doctor in thanks
And welcome and amusement.
                                    If Doctor Moor
Had come to say again to John in summer
What he had said in winter, he did not say it.
Sun, that friend to haymakers and sweat,
Is not a friend to the giving of good advice,
Even the wisest or the friendliest.
John had the look of a man who knows he is safe
From any assault of friend or enemy
In heaven above or earth beneath or the waters
Under the earth. The superfluity,
The delicious superfluity of doctors!

The doctor's smile could have been read to mean:
Superfluous? Who mentioned doctor at all?
What shred of damaging evidence today?

So grinning, they shook hands.
                                        We won't unload
Till after dinner, John said. It must be noon.
You'll eat with us of course.
                                    They stood awhile,

The three, watching the hayrick dip and rock
Over the rough ground like a galleon,
Sylvester navigating from the bridge,
While over his head and over the hills great clouds
Were a surf along the wide beach of the sky.

Leif made an upward circle of his arms,
Lifting them sidewise till the fingers touched,
Then brought his clasped hands down upon his head,
And so stood looking.
                              Now for our dip, John said.
Have you seen our inland sea?
                              Leif led the way
To a brook that ran out of the woods as fast
As if it had been running away from woods.
Before it ran down hill and so was lost
It had to fill a pool that they had dug—
The nearest Valhalla ever came to Ocean.

There in the open sunlight John and Leif
Slipped off their shoes and trousers. John stepped in,
Shouting from the shock of cold, and ducked.
Leif (for the water was not deep enough
For diving) ran and jumped in with a splash
That made the pool a momentary fountain.

The doctor had taken off his outer shirt
And was dashing handfuls of water on face and arms.

Sun and wind and hands were towels enough.
As they stood there drying, turning now this side,
Now that side to the sun (Leif innocent
Of any thought about himself, his father
Aware of self yet clean of embarrassment),
The doctor made no effort to conceal
His privilege of looking where he pleased.
However unprofessionally he joked
And laughed, his glance was searching, impersonal,
A doctor's. Having satisfied himself
With the look of Leif's appendicitis scar,
He studied the whole boy, who did not see
He was being studied.—How every line and impulse
Of docile body expressed what was not body,

And how the boy expressed the father too.
Seeing them thus together, he saw the boy
More clearly in the man, the man in the boy.

He saw beyond identities, no longer
Leif and his father, but the anonymous
Generic human body, genus homo,
Elaborate ingenuity of nature,
Yet sad, absurd, grotesque.
                                There came an instant
He almost saw, had felt the threat and was saved
From seeing something obscene, misshapen, monstrous,
Something fished from the mile-deep midnight ocean—
A pale and mutilated octopus.

Almost—if one of the bodies had not moved
In a certain way in time and saved them both—
And John and Leif standing there in the sun.

Where is your ship, Leif? Doctor Moor was asking.
I thought this was the sea where you go sailing.

Leif looked up quickly at the asker, his eyes
Telling how much there was he couldn't say.

Leif used to have a ship, his father said.
You must admit a sea is rather small
For a man to sail in when it's cramped for swimming.

The two men looked at each other as men do
Over the implication of a fact—
A just perceptible narrowing of the eyes—
While Leif was busy with his shoes and trousers.

I like your arrangement here, the doctor said.
With a wave of his hand as if to indicate
The arrangement of the earth and sky and Valhalla
Among the other mountains. Take this morning
For instance. You spend it haying, a pleasant way
To spend a morning. But even if it weren't
What better introduction to this water?
Then once cooled off and clean, one thinks of dinner
And lo and behold, the dinner is forthcoming.

I say I like your arrangement.
                        So do we
Laughed John.
                And what does dinner introduce?

More haying.

                Then more splashing, then more eating?

Then some sleeping. That's how we arrange it.

In other words, the doctor went on gravely,
You plan to spend all of your time in living?
(Leif smiled to see the others keep from smiling.)

We calculate there will be time enough
For other things when we are dead, said John.

Why die at all? (That made Leif laugh outright.)
Why not arrange to live for ever and ever?

Plenty of people have planned precisely that,
John said. I never heard you praise them for it.

Ah, but they weren't inhabitants of heaven.
As you are here. Isn't this heaven, Leif?
Valhalla? Where is heaven if this is somewhere
Else?
        Leif hasn't come to heaven yet
In his geography, John interposed.
He has studied only solid earth thus far,
Particularly this hill, this part of Vermont,
And most particularly of all of course
The seven seas that might have touched Vermont
But didn't. Another flaw in our arrangement.

Leif knew that this was fooling and something more,
But he didn't know (the way he smiled showed that)
Where one left off and where the other began.
But did it matter if he didn't know
At noontime on a day in mid-July,
Half of the day to east and half to west,
The world to east and west and north and south,

Still cool from water, warm and dry in sun,
Hungry for dinner and dinner almost ready?

These peas were grown in Eden's sweetpea garden,
Said John. Doubtless you taste the difference.

I do. I certainly do, the doctor said,
Dipping a spoonful, playing the connoisseur.

May I tell something, Mother, Johanna whispered,
About the peas? The colors, I mean, and the seasons?
You see, the peas are green for spring and summer.
The cream that Ruth put in is white for winter.
The butter was yellow autumn, before it melted.

So when you eat the peas you eat the year.
The whole year in one dish, the doctor added.
I wonder, does making food mean other things
Improve the taste of it?
                                        Of course it does.

Such ripe conviction from a child so small,
Such readiness to defend imagination
Against a doubting world, would have made him laugh
If her blue eyes had been less earnest.
                                                    Of course
It does, he reproached himself. Of course it does.

We like peas raw too, right out of the pod,
Leif said. We like to shell them into our mouths,
Eden and Jan and I.
                          That makes you rabbits,
Doesn't it? Doesn't that make you rabbits or deer?
Eden and Leif laughed with him. Johanna's face
Was like a flower that the wind in a field
Stirring the other flowers fails to stir.

Doesn't it? he insisted in a tone
That was half-uncertain of its playfulness,
A tone and way of looking into her eyes
To make her smile or to discover the reason
For not smiling. But all that he could see
In those clear eyes, but could not read, was a question

Touched with fear.
                        He glanced from child to mother,
Seeing that moment how the children's laughter
And all their graver moods derived from her.

Across the room from open window to window
Faintly a breeze felt only on the face
That blended warmth with coolness.
                              Warmth of bread
Fresh from the baking and the coolness of milk,
And clouds whose whiteness makes the blue sky bluer,
And early blossoms and hay ripe for the harvest.
Thinking of warmth and coolness the older man
Was silent, and the children too were still.

                    .   .   .

August brought days when there were hills of heat
Upon the other hills, and summer apples
Were heavy on the trees. A few had fallen.
Eden compared the flavor of one from the tree
With one from the ground. Then feeling heavy with heat
Herself she slipped her light dress off, and sighed,
And touched a fallen apple with her toe
Tentatively, then poked it out of her way,
And sighed again and lay down in the grass
Under a tree.
              The apples over her head
Were Damoclean danger just enough
For her to enjoy. She lay there looking up,
With hands clasped now behind her head and now
Over a lifted knee. This was the place
Where months before she had lain and let the blossoms
Drift over her. She smiled remembering
The tickle of the petals that had touched her,
And how she had watched them fall trying to guess
Which would alight on her and which on grass.
Eden was in the mood for comparisons
But if she ever thought to compare herself
Either to petals or to summer apples
(And there was something to be said for both)
The thought came lightly as a little fly
And flew away.
              Another thing came lightly

Too if it came at all, and that was sleep.
A suddenly dimmed and sunless world was round her
As if the hours of afternoon were lost
And twilight come, till looking up through leaves
She saw looming above the tree above her
A thunderhead cut out of solid white
Carved in a thousand curves crowding the sky.
So dragon-headed and measureless a thing
To move so soundlessly.
                                    Eden sat up.
A shiver in the grass made her glance down
And see a disappearing piece of black
Like dead-ripe blackberries or wet charred wood.

She jumped up, shuddered, then saw the other black
In the western sky, flashing its forked fire tongue.
And as it came it swallowed up the hills.

There was a black snake once that robbed a cow
Of milk, Eden had heard Sylvester say
When she had been supposed to be too small
To remember things. Could it be true? Ruth asked.
But asking could it be true had made it true.
The farmer noticing the milk was short,
Hid in the pasture to see who was the thief.
After a while he saw a great black snake
That glided over the ground and up to the cow
And reared its head and looked this way and that
And then began to milk her like a calf.
Hissing himself the farmer killed the snake.
Go kill the cow! the farmer's wife commanded.
Would anybody want to drink *her* milk?

Eden could feel a faint breath on her body
And apple leaves about her felt it too.
Far in the west the red tongue flashed again
And licked the top of a mountain. Eden shivered.
She stooped and picked her dress up, put it on
And ran down from the orchard.
                                    Beyond the barn
Sylvester stood bareheaded and impartial,
Estimating the power of the storm.
He calculated distance, time, direction.

He looked prepared for anything to come
Whenever it came.
                    If it weren't for thunderstorms,
Sylvester, life might be a little tame,
Especially in summer. (This from John.)
Vermont has no volcanoes active now,
Seldom an earthquake, never a tidal wave.
What would we do without our thunderstorms?
They make a bluff at least at being bad.

They're mostly firecrackers, muttered Sylvester.
Mostly Fourth of July. On land, that is.
At sea—
        The thunder interrupted him.
They heard the storm-sigh of Valhalla trees.

A storm at sea is another thing from a storm
On land. Are your mountains rock or are they water?

Wind blew away the words, Or are they water?
It was the wind they had been waiting for.
It shivered green leaves silver on the trees,
And dead leaves, some of last year's in the grass
It caught up in the air with living birds
And coiled them together.
                        Imitating birds
Or leaves or sails or anything the wind
Will blow Leif let himself be blown about
The pasture in wide circles, while Johanna
Was imitating leaves and birds and Leif.
With widely lifted arms they ran and wheeled
And dipped and soared and almost left the ground.
And all the while they wailed and moaned wind-wise.
Their circling heads shone all the paler-brighter
Beneath the ragged black scud racing above them.
A semi-circle of original blue
Far in the east was all the blue sky left.
The west was rain itself, rain visible
In silver rushing veils over the valley.

John and Sylvester had gone indoors at last.
What birds had not been blown away were in hiding.
Lightning shook a finger at the hill:

You're next. And thunder backed the lightning up.
But still the children skimmed about like swallows
Over a marsh or meadow, until they felt
The first big drops splash on their palms and faces,
Then swooped down into the house with the sudden curve
Of chimney-swifts.
                    Behind them when they turned
They saw the hill was blind with rain and lightning,
Two blindnesses—darkness and too much light.
Thunder was mountains splitting and granite halves
Of mountains grinding together. They loved it loud.
The rain was coming in waves for the wind was rhythmic.
They watched them loom and blur and billow by
And the trees bow down, or were they bending backwards,
Laughing at rain, shaking their shining hair?

And they were watching at that tingling moment
Valhalla turned white noon and winter stars.
Almost before they saw they heard it coming—
Sound of someone starting to rip a cloth
Or the sky, then with a jerk rip it apart.

John ran outdoors and disappeared in rain.
Edith ran after, was it to close the door?
She hesitated with her hand on the knob,
The rush of rain-cool sweetness against her face.
She stood there in the open doorway waiting.

Lightning was fainter now and thunder farther.
Whatever they had had to do to the hill
Had been done. But rain had something more to do.
Big, crowding, it hit the hissing round
With a downward wind. If one could judge from the sight
And sound of it, the rain was in a hurry.
And John laughing at how much rain one man
Could bring back without trying into the house,
Brushing it from his hair and out of his eyes
To see hardly needed to say, Everything safe.
Only a tree perhaps.
                    (They did not see
Johanna's eyes go wider at the words.)

Let's take off our clothes and run in the rain, Leif shouted.
Hurry, hurry, while it's coming hard.

Ready himself, not waiting for his sisters,
He poised a moment as a diver does
About to take a running dive, and ran
Out through the doorway.
                              If rain had been a river
Leif would have swum in it. He did his best
As it was by flinging his arms and leaping high.

The sisters having slipped off their moods with their dresses,
Joined hands with Leif, Johanna in the center.
The three began to race (all three would win)
Out over the pasture-sea. They splashed the puddles
To surf, and the grass was seaweed under their feet.
Farther and farther they ran till they became
To those that watched them run a moving color.

The blessed fishes, Ruth breathed aloud to herself.
Ruth had no word for anything half-fish,
Half-human, never having heard of Naiads,
Nereids and Nixies. But she knew the sheen
And suppleness of trout and pickerel.

Still hand in hand they swung about,
Leif bracing himself as pivot, and started back.
They watched the rain as they ran instead of the ground,
Letting the little pools surprise their feet.
They knew the storm would soon be over now
By the way it fell in soft, glistening flakes.

But old Sylvester trudging out to pasture
Seemed with his rubber boots and overalls
To be a thing the storm had left behind.
He did not pause or smile or turn as they passed.
He pretended not to see them or hear their laughter,
Though it was less at him than at themselves.

What could be weighing on an old man's mind?

Oh, Mother, we have been miles and miles and miles
Out in the rain. Almost around the world.

And Edith feeling Johanna's little body
Throb in the towel that she held around her,
Looked down into her face, smoothed back her hair,
And said the same words, Almost around the world.

The sun flashed out. A few raindrops still fell.
A puddle here and there a patch of grass,
Then all the grass and all the hill grew bright,
Faded, brightened again. A new clear day
Beginning in the west before the night.
Another season coming with the night.
The sky was evidence wherever sky
Could show—that color, coolness, quality.

Then in the doorway blocking radiance
Sylvester stood and looked at them and waited
For breath to speak. The grayness of his face
Was a thing they had never rightly seen before.

John waited for him.
                    The elm, Sylvester began.

The lightning struck it? John asked in a tone
In which the statement overruled the question.

Struck it and streaked its side. Sylvester paused.
Under the tree, he said.
                    Under the tree,
John finished for him Audhumbla must have been standing.

The high hushed voices of the children crying,
Audhumbla?
                    No one needed to name the thing.
They saw an old man standing in the doorway,
His face in shadow but behind his head
The suddenly blinding sun about to set.

IV

The valley sees the pasture on the hill.
Below the pasture and above are woods
Up to the wooded peak up to the sky.
The valley sees the darkness of evergreens
Waiting above the pasture to come down
As other evergreens have come or wait
To come to darken pastures on other hills.

Anything more than this is for the hunters
Fall and winter, or children in July
Blueberrying among the junipers.
They see a little more but only a little,
Too busy with the blue under their hands
To bother with the blue over their heads,
Yet drifting nearer and nearer that bluer blue.

Sometimes a boy on such a blueberry day
Little by little will wander up so far
That before he knows it he is near the cow,
The one white cow poised near the pasture crest.
He hears her rhythmic grazing before he thinks
To look up from his pail. A little while
He watches her, then gets up from his knees,
Stretches himself and looks down over the valley
To where he lives and tries to find his house
And wonders if anyone at home can see him.
But no one sees him there, not even his mother
Though she knows where to look and more than once
That afternoon has looked up at the hill.
Does it seem far to her for him to be?

Did it seem far to her that afternoon?
And did it still in after years seem far?
Evenings when she sat by her lamp alone,
Sewing, sewing, her needle never resting,
Sewing until her hair was white in the lamplight,
Did far become less far and near less near?

May and warm and the window open wide.
She sat listening to the sounds outside
Of leaf-stir, distant voices, a barking dog,
And all the indistinguishable sounds
Of night. Nearby the sound of ticking time.
And then the sound of footsteps in the house.

Judd?
          I'm going to bed. I'm tired, he said.

She heard him on the stairs. She heard his door,
And heard him moving about his room above.
Then everything was still except the clock
Indoors and out of doors the leaves, the voices,

So much a boy to be so much a man
With his shop, his printer's sign, his business card,
The roll of dollar bills in his pocketbook
(Mother, do you need any money today?)
And his hands giving the money, his printer's hands
With fingernails that never could be clean.

There was the little boy who played so hard
He used to fall asleep before his bedtime—
Before he grew to be that other boy
Begging to stay up after bedtime. And now,
Tonight, before it was time to light the lamps,
I'm tired, I'm going to bed.
                              She heard his voice.
Was he talking to himself awake or dreaming?
His pillow mornings when she made his bed
Was proof of dreams, but the pillow never told her
What the dreams were.
                      Not even he was sure
Always when he awoke how much was dream,
How much remembered. What he did remember
After these months was the sting, the giddiness,
How he had had to shut his eyes for strength
To see again, and the sudden taste in his mouth.

Naked, nothing hidden or withheld
From him, yet all oblivious of him,
Color of sunlight, blossom, fruit—the girl

Under the apple trees and looking up.
And he rigid within the edge of woods,
His hand grasping a tree, a heaviness
Like death upon him.
                        Slowly he had drawn back
Watching to see that he was still unseen
With every step unheard into the woods,
Then running, stumbling, escaping down the hill.

Why had he ever started toward the hill
That August afternoon when he closed his shop
And hung the sign on the door that said Return,
And told himself it was too hot to work?
Why had he not gone down to the river swimming?
Wet and weak from the heat and running, why
Had he stopped and turned and climbed all the way again
And found the place and looked and found her gone?

She was always somewhere in his mind, and gone,
Though sometimes something more of her would come
To him out of whiteness—his pillow when he woke,
The paper in his press before it was printed.
Farther and farther back he followed her.
Was she the sister of the little one
He still could see across a supper table?
And when on blueberry days in blueberry years
He had hidden behind some junipers to watch
Three sunlit children (he could remember three)
Bare in the sun and wind—could she have been one?

The sign said Closed, Return, but did not say
When the return would be. Judd did not know.
The woods were heavy with leaves, the gloom, the sound.
Above the leaves the birds of the insect voices
Soliloquizing all a summer day.
And above the birds the clouds that climb the sky.
Not much was there to interrupt a mood
Or make one stop except perhaps the sudden
White of mountain laurel.
                        Judd did not stop.
Not even where the woodroad passed near ledges
From which he might have looked back over the valley.
He was thirsty but he did not think of water

Although the leaves sounded like distant rivers.

Before it entered the pasture he left the road
But kept close to the pasture all the way
To see and not be seen. Only once he stopped—
It was a little bush of mountain laurel
Compact and pink in the sunshine. Then he went on.

The dark trees on the peak, the pointed spruces,
Seem to those who see them always the same—
Dark in summer, dark in winter, dark
And undisturbed from year to year by fall
Or wind or rain or frost or snow or spring.
They keep the peak, holding and held by rock,
Holding and fed by soil once tree and rock.
So they endure.
                    The hill is higher for them
But was not high enough for Leif grown tall,
Tall as his father. So they built a tower.
They felled four spruces, cleared them of limbs and bark
And rooted them a second time in rock.
They bound the four together, and built a ladder
Up to the top. The work took months and strength
Leif had not known he had, and gave him strength.
His ax grew light. What his father did Leif did.

What did a watcher on the tower see?
A few miles farther. At night a few more stars.
There were nights they called by name all the stars they knew,
And other nights when Leif on the tower alone
Searched the North Star to find its difference.

But seeing more and farther was less to them
Than seeing their own Valhalla from above,
The hawk's way. Tracing those patterns of dark and light,
The evergreens among the summer trees.
They saw their farm as something outside themselves.
They could compare its place on the hill with places
Where other farms had been in other years,
Pastures once, now grown or partly grown
To evergreen.
                    Progress or retrogress—
They saw time moving over the hill from age

To age, from summer to fall to winter to spring,
From day to night.
                    After those first months
When the tower had often drawn the five together,
They went alone according to their mood
As they had the time or happened to be near.
Drawing them one by one it had to draw them
(However imperceptibly) apart.

Johanna always climbed the ladder slowly
As if the going up among the trees
Were growing up with them. To see a bough
Above, and watch above become below.
To pause there halfway and forgetting higher.
So quietly that once she reached the top
Before she found that Eden was up there reading.

Leif read on rainy days. He had his work
And visits to the tower were part of it.
It needed repair perhaps, or watching in wind.
If it were ever going to crash in wind
(Though there was nothing to make him think it would)
He wanted to be up there, on top, and go
When the tower went, swinging away to a spruce.

In wind the tower felt alive beneath him,
Like standing barefoot on a horse's back
(As he had done), or standing with legs braced
On a ship's bridge (as he had never done).
For gulls there were crows and hawks and sometimes a heron
Buffeted or blown across the hill.
It was the distant bird Leif watched the longest,
The last hill out, the farthest gleam of water.

A few of the upper leaves were water-silver.
The air was moving just enough for that.
Haze had erased the hills, the farther ones.
A day for the snake on the ground, not for the bird.

Leif couldn't think of anything to do
Or to want to do. What had been done, what left?
He couldn't tell why he had come to the tower
That afternoon, or what there was to see

87

Worth seeing. The world had shrunk. All other worlds
Were out of sight.
                         He turned to go, but turning
Saw in an interval of heavy woods
On the off side of the hill, a girl's dress, Eden.
And then another color, dark, a man.
Only a moment the two were there together.
Then one was lost in trees and then the other.

Somewhere in the world of August heat
The cream had soured. When would the storm be coming?

He glided down the ladder. One thing was clear:
Direction. There was a woodroad leading there
Noiseless almost with moss and evergreen needles.
Leif hurried slowly, listening to sounds
(The lesser birds and breezes, little more)
And listening for sounds he did not hear.

A hemlock grove is a hiding place for night
In day, for deer in winter, for snow in spring.
But Leif had never hidden behind dark trees
Except in playing hide-and-seek as a child.
Now he was both the hider and the seeker.

They came, the stranger and Eden, Eden strange
Herself, walking alone, and he the shadow.
They went as two will go who have gone that way
Before.
          Leif was a tree till they were past,
A birch among the hemlocks, a tree with eyes,
And then with feet, lightly and darkly moving.

Once Eden, scarcely pausing, stooped to pick,
It might have been a leaf, a spear of grass.

Where the woodroad forked, one leading to the farm,
The other down the hill, he drew her to him.
Both fear and willingness were in her face,
The upturned face like that of a drowning girl.

They drew apart but only far enough
For each to see the other. Eden turned

To go, looked back at him then hurried away.
He waited till the trees had taken her.

Leif watched the watcher till he too had gone.
That instant he was the arrow flying after.
Hearing a sound, Judd turned and saw him coming.
He stood his ground. Leif stopped. No question spoken.
The one word, Snake! Then fists. The trees closed in.
Two worlds. One would be saved, the other lost.

And Leif was losing. With all his strength of fists,
Shoulder and lungs, he had never fought before.
Whom had there ever been before to fight?

Bewildered by the blows he failed to land,
Bewildered by the blows the other landed,
Sobbing with anger, struggle, failure, shame,
He sprang back trying to see his way to fight.
But what he saw was blood on the other's fists.
No father's eyes forbidding him to fall.
The light dimmed and went out.

                                        The trees stood round.
They murmured, but their murmuring said nothing.
They trembled, but their trembling was the air
In motion. What was this light and dark to them
Whose life was storm and sunlight, day and darkness?
They didn't care.
                        The birds cared even less.
They didn't stop their feeding for a moment.
They flitted from bough to bough or flew away.

Opening his eyes Leif saw a face above him.
Someone was fanning him. He closed his eyes.
But when he opened them again and looked,
There was no one there. He raised himself on an elbow
Trying to find a reason for his weakness.
Waveringly he stood. Then he remembered.

No weight he ever lifted or tried to lift
Was heavy as this weight of remembering.
He felt himself go down with it, and wanted
To go where there could be no farther falling.

Not thinking where he went or caring where
He came to the pool that once had been his sea.
He knelt, lay down, and hid his face in grass.

He could remember hearing long ago
Of a man who went to a field beside a stream
And held his face in water until he drowned.

Leif crawled to the pool and let his head hang over
And saw himself, or was it himself, in water.
There was a moment when he looked at death,
Looked on the face and into the eyes of death,
And willing to look deeper. But the cool
Ambiguous water was not death this time.
He drew his head out of the pool and breathed.

.   .   .

The first cool nights at last, the turn toward winter
With fruit still growing bigger on the trees
And the air still sweet with the flower-fruit of corn.
A cool hand over the warm body of summer,
Touch and excitement of the two together,
The tower waiting for him.
                                But Leif wasn't there.
Not on the tower. Eden wasn't there.
And neither ever asked where the other was.
Together in a room they had a way
Of seeing everything except each other.
They had the look of seeming to see too much.

Johanna had supposed as a little girl
That when she was as old as Leif had been
When his ax was new, she could always go with him
Wherever he went and be wherever he was.
She had supposed so being a little girl.

Trees were her friends. They never were too busy
To listen to anything she had to say,
Or whisper confidences of their own.
So many friends—she ought to have been content.

One afternoon on the tower too clear for earth,
No cloud in the sky, no bird, the trees green metal,

Johanna felt the hill slip back an age,
Or was it forward? And she the only one
Who saw and was. No farm was there, no man,
No woman, child. She was the last or first.

.   .   .

The morning sun too dazzling, shadows too sharp.
Hearing a step and glancing up from his printing
Judd had to shade his eyes to see in the doorway
Someone standing. Could it be Eden's brother?
The figure stepped inside, and then he saw.

I've come to see you, Judd.
                              Judd did not speak.

I've come to see what you intend to do.
They stood there separated by a knife
The sun thrust through the window to the floor.
Judd waited for the other to make a move
Or speak again. But the other waited too.

Judd lowered his hand from his eyes. What do you mean?
(Trying to make the words sound like a question.)

I mean Eden, Eden's father answered.
He stepped toward Judd across and through the knife.
Blood was the answer's answer in Judd's face.

Eden is pregnant. You knew that of course?

I didn't know it, he said, and swallowed shame.

What is your plan?
                    I haven't any plan.

You haven't any plan, but I have one.
I came to you today. You come to me
Tomorrow. Come with your plan. Come in the morning.
This is your invitation and your summons.
You understand?
                  I understand, said Judd.

No more was said. The other turned and went.

Judd sat down on his printer's stool at last.
The only motion that he made was breathing.

She heard him come indoors and climb the stairs
And no good night. His steps tried to be soft
To let her know he didn't want to be seen
Or spoken to or even thought about.

But what had she to do but think of him
Until she sighed and laid her sewing down
And went to bed?
      She must have gone to sleep
And waked, hearing him talking overhead
As if there were not one of him but two.
After it ceased, she lay there listening
Until a rooster crowed too loud too early.

The words were Closed, Return. A morning mist
That separates one clear day from another
Was reason for not looking far ahead
Or back as he went up the dripping woodroad.

John met him at the door. Come in, sit down.

I want to marry Eden.
      Then you have asked her?
The question was quick. So was the answer, No,
But I love her and I know that she loves me.

Love is an ambiguous word, said John.
A man may love the woman that he steals from.
That is one way of loving, a common way.

Judd stood up rigid, smarting.
      John did not stir.
The question is how deep and far do you love?
Another question, What has your love to live on?
Loving is easier than earning a living.

You mean you think I couldn't support a wife?
You think I haven't the money? Look at that!
And he thrust his open pocketbook toward John.
That's what I earn and I can earn more like it.

Loving is easier than earning a living
Is it? Maybe it is, but I can do both.

John got up from his chair and went to a window.
Whatever he saw outside seemed something clear.

Money is hard or money is easy to earn.
But there are harder things than money to give.
What would you do if you became convinced
That Eden could be happy only here
On this hill where she has lived since she was five?

Judd frowned. Why should I be convinced of that?

Would you be willing to live where she was happy?

Judd's frown deepened. I'm a printer, he said.
My work's down there. I earn my living there.
God, but you're hard, as hard and smooth as glass.
Everything, everything looks so clear to you.
But nothing's clear, I tell you. Happiness!
Who's happy anyhow? Is Eden happy?
How do you know? Can you see happiness
By looking out the window?
                              As if the sound
Of her name had summoned her, she was standing there
Within the doorway—visionary, grave
And still as someone standing in a dream,
A walker in her sleep, and they afraid
To wake her.
              Eden?
                      She looked at her father.
                                              Eden?
I heard, she said. I knew what you would say.
But why is this the only place to live?
Don't people live on other hills and where
There are no hills? Even the birds that live here
Go and come and some of them come back.
Why shouldn't I go as well?
                              There was no answer.

She turned toward Judd as if he were a stranger
Across the room, and saw him watching her

As if she too were strange. She went to him.
She stood before him, arms limp at her side.
Ghost to ghost they might have been until
A flush appeared in his eyes. She saw it there
And knew that hers had made acknowledgment.
And then his arms around her and his lips
(No ghost's acknowledgment) against her lips.

.   .   .

There is no line, no boundary, no mark,
No first leaf falling, no first bird flying south.
We know what happens after it is done,
Sometimes the end, never the beginning.
If birds that go tried to conceal their going
They could not do much better than they do.
A few at a time. We never know the time
Ahead, or if we happen to see them go
We do not know if they have gone for good
Or will come back. We never say good-bye.

Eden's going in autumn was like autumn
Gradual. Her thoughts flew on ahead
Bird-like, a few at a time, and some would return.
We do not say good-bye to birds or thoughts.

And yet there came a day for saying good-bye.
They stood outdoors in the sun. A little wind
Was over the hill, a few leaves drifting down.
It was time to go. Eden and Judd were ready.
Sun and pride were color in his face,
Pride of the fighter who has fought and won.
They saw, they understood, they gave consent,
Acknowledging defeat. And Edith could smile
A little for Eden's sake without pretense.

Who were the people, they had used to ask
The children long ago, who lived in the land
Beyond the moon where no one ever smiled?
When any child was out of sorts or sad
Or over-solemn, they would ask him that.
Edith wanted to ask the question now.

The shadow of a white-owl cloud swooped down

Over the hill, and it was nearer night
And winter for a moment. Far away
A train was hooting softly in the valley.

Johanna was the last to say good-bye.
She looked up in Judd's face, seeming intent
On something necessary, final, strange.
He guessed, leaned down and turned his cheek to her
And smiled as he felt her little frightened kiss.

V

Not mist, not rain, not even a rainy night
Could shut the hill in like the fall of snow,
Hushing all sounds except its own, hiding
Both ground and sky, even remembered sky.

Inside the storm, inside her stall in the barn
Audhumbla may have heard the scarcely audible
Scratching of flakes against the little window
And felt the chill but could not see the snow.
Hay was her world, her fodder, bedding, fragrance.
All the snow that fell or was to fall
That winter would not last as long as hay.

Coming from whiteness cold to whiteness warm,
Audhumbla's breath and body, loving the cold
And warm together, the sense of being in snow
Yet sheltered, Johanna would often come and stand
Within the aura of heat around the cow.

Audhumbla, did you know that it was snowing?
Look at me, Audhumbla, you old white cow.
I'm whiter than you are, whiter that is in spots.
I'm older than you are too, though who would believe it?
Sometimes it seems there never was a time
When you were not Audhumbla. I almost forget
You're not Audhumbla the first but only the second.
No, not the second, the third, at least the third.
The first one was a very different cow
From you or any cow you ever saw.
All that she had to eat was salt and frost
She licked from stones. Now how would you like that?

Her milk, as you might suppose, was melting snow.
There couldn't have been much cream, could there, Audhumbla?
But then, there was no one there to drink the milk
Except one giant. People hadn't been born.
And that's the cow, Audhumbla, you were named for.
Audhumbla, are you listening? Are you? Are you?

Snow that could hide one world could bring another
Nearer, world of the first, the far Valhalla
Even for Leif who hated make-believe.

The steepest slope was best, at least for him.
And what was best for him was best for Johanna.
Whatever he did, she did. Tracks of his skis
And hers ran parallel or coincided.
The way to be with him was to follow him.
The way to be at the foot when he swerved and slid
Magnificently in a foam of snow to a stand
And turned and shouted to her, How did you like it,
Jan? was to take the same sharp slope herself.

And there were the Valkyries. They helped her too.
However mythical their stirruped feet,
They steadied her own thighs and knees and ankles.
They helped to keep her up in going down.
Leif never wanted to wait. A few deep breaths,
An impatient stamping of skis on the packed snow,
And then the long climb up. Johanna was ready.
The climbing up was never too steep with Leif.

Audhumbla, you wouldn't know your pasture now
If you were there. I hardly know it myself.
You wouldn't know me either with my skis.
You'd think I was a kind of rabbit-bird.
Audhumbla, Audhumbla, will you promise something?
Promise me you'll always be the same,
Audhumbla, and I'll promise you the same.

· · ·

The overlapping intermingling season
Of winter-spring when anyone is free
To call the weather either, neither, or both

According as he feels, and speak the truth.
Birds coming back, snow going, but more to come.
Coldness and warmth clinging to each other
Like wrestlers wrestling for the fun of it,
Now one, now the other getting the upper hand.
Such was the time when Eden's boy was born.

Are babies very very beautiful, Ruth?

Beautiful? Newborn babies beautiful?
(Ruth finished pinning a napkin to the line.)
You ought to have seen yourself when you were born.

I didn't mean myself, Johanna said.
But Eden—wasn't she a beautiful baby?

Not to begin with. You may be sure of that.

Johanna watched Ruth feel the sheets on the line
Billowing and ballooning in the wind
To see how near they were to dry.
                                I wonder—
Johanna said, and that was all she said.

A day to start the grass and stir the seed
And make a rooster crow, and crowd both mind
And body (Leif's eighteen-year-old mind and body)
And make a hill too cramped a place to live.

Father and son were splitting wood together
Making their axes ring antiphonally.

John paused for breath, and Leif paused also,
                                        Father,
I think the time has come for me to go.
He waited for the thing his father would say.

I think so too.
                It caught Leif unprepared.
He had no answer.
                        The axes paused again.

Your uncle, you'll go to him of course, said John.

He'll show you parts of the world that can't be seen
From here. When you come back we'll still be here.
The hill will be here.
                    They went on with their work.

Another day when they were together again
John said, If you're back in time for haying, good.
If not, we'll manage a summer without you somehow.
Go when it's time and come when it's time, but remember,
Leif, your mother has had you eighteen years.
While you're away she'll have the letters you write.

The time when trees that flower before they leave
Were in flower, willows, alders, maples, elms,
Earlier flowers than all but a few of the ground.
Now flowers of elm were over Johanna's head.
Of all the times she had stood beneath this tree
(Standing with it because it stood alone,
Seeing with it all that it might have seen)
There were two, and one of them was years ago
When she had waited here to see Leif come.
And other was now, waiting to see him go.

This was the real good-bye, after the words.
The last look. And would he think to turn
And look back at the hill? And if he did
Would he see the elm and see her standing there?

Once, twice the whistle of a train—
The loneliest sound within the hollow world
Johanna had ever heard. She put her hand
Against the tree to feel the rough-ridged bark
With her fingertips and moved her hand along
Until it touched and knew the lightning scar,
But she never looked away from the valley road.

                .   .   .

Her father stood in her garden one day in June
Looking at the impeccable pattern of greens,
Serious-minded, sober vegetable greens
In geometric rows—lettuce, spinach,
Beans, carrots, cabbage, even potatoes,
And not one weed and not one flower either.

The leaves were lovely as the leaves of flowers
But loveliness was not their reason here.
He thought of Eden's garden years ago,
Sweetpeas. There were no sweetpeas in Johanna's garden.
John stood looking. There was more to see
Than vegetables in strict unerring rows
If one had wit to read between the rows.

It was the same with haying in July.
In other years Johanna had hayed a little
Partly to help, partly for fun, and mostly
Because Leif let her take his fork for a while.
Now it was all work. She worked till dinner
And after dinner all the afternoon.
If she was tired, she didn't let it be known.

Why I don't see, Sylvester said to John,
But what she does as well as a boy of her age.
Better than some boys do.
                              John answered nothing.

Sylvester started for the barn with the load,
The last load for the day. John turned to Johanna.
Wisps of hair were wet about her face.
A trickle down one cheek. She looked at her father
With not the slightest wish for pity or praise.

Go to the pool and have a good old splash.
Sylvester and I can do the unloading alone.

If in his look of approval there was a hint
Of disapproval, Johanna saw it, felt it.
She understood. She couldn't fill Leif's place.
But when would he come back to take his place?

The pool, his pool, was empty of any answer.
Only the water and a few reflections—
Marginal grass and clouds and a girl's plain face
Gazing up at her.
                    Leif's letters didn't tell.
They told of things of which she had never dreamed.
And always the ocean. How he had seen it, swum in it,
Sailed on it. Statement of fact was eloquent.

99

Eden's letters were interwoven with Leif's
Like strands of music. Little Judd was growing,
Getting a tooth and then another tooth.
Eden's love was something visible
And bright and warm like her long hair in sunlight.

After supper during the summertime
Edith would sometimes take her chair outdoors
And sit sewing as long as she could see.
Johanna would bring her chair and sew beside her.

One evening as it grew darker Edith said
(She didn't look away from her sewing to say it)
Jan dear, I've been thinking of something pleasant.
I'd like (she paused with her needle) to make you a dress,
A prettier dress than any you've ever had.

But Mother, do I need a new dress now?

Oh, let's not talk of need. Life's not all need.
I'd love to make it if you'd love to wear it.

Both sewed silently a little while.

When would I wear it, Mother?
                              Anytime
That you were specially happy. Leif would like it.

When he comes home, I could wear it for him then.

Edith lay down her sewing. It was too dark
To see.
        When he comes home, you could wear it then.

A wind like early fall and a whitecap letter
From Leif. I have a job on a sailing ship.
Just what it was he didn't bother to say.
We're off on a cruise. I don't know exactly where
Or just how long we'll be gone. I'll write when I can.
I'll tell you all about it when I get home.
At last.
        They wondered over that At last.

John thought it meant At last I've reached the sea,
While Edith thought At last when I am home.
Johanna trying to reconcile the two
Said Couldn't At last mean both? Both sea and home?

The wind was making waves of the tops of trees
As Edith went up through the woods to the peak.
She had the sense of walking under the sea.
And when she came to the tower and climbed to the top,
It was like a diver's coming to the surface
Out of the dark green depths. Why had she come?
Why had she made a secret of her coming?

Full in the wind, feeling the tower sway,
She thought how wide a thing was wind blowing
Both clouds that went with it and trees that staid,
Making no distinction of great and small,
Near and far, land and sea. And thoughts,
Were they more like clouds in the wind or more like trees?

She went down out of the wind through evergreens.
No one had seen her go or saw her come.

Leif's next letter came from the Caribbean.
Bound for further south. Everything well.
They found the places on the globe, the ports
Where he had touched, the islands. They followed his ship.
They saw the sea brilliant and blue, and something
More: a certain shape to his sentences,
Fulfilment. So long as he was sailing south
Winter would never freeze some things on the hill.

To think I've lived close on to seventy year,
Sylvester said while he was milking Audhumbla,
Seventy year, and never seen the sea.

I've never seen it either, said Johanna.

He milked a while in silence, the only sound.
The streams of milk striking within the pail.

Sylvester, if Father is willing would you be willing

101

EL CAMINO COLLEGE
LIBRARY

To let me do the milking—all the time,
I mean?
            You think I'm getting too old for it?

Not yet, Sylvester, but you will be sometime.

Milking is not a woman's proper work.

Sometimes women have to do men's work.

His milking done, he stood up, took his pail,
And started out.
                Sylvester?
                        He stopped, turned.

Did you ever think how many things there are
That I can't do, perhaps can never do?
But I know how to milk Audhumbla, don't I?

He had no answer. Turned and trudged away.

Day after day with a stuff as blue as the sea
Spread out before her Edith had been sewing,
And now the dress was done. Trying it on
Johanna said she was putting on the sea.

I'll wear it first when Leif comes back, in spring.

But won't that be too long to wait? asked Ruth.

No, said Johanna, if I have to wait.
Wishing the time away won't make it go.

Ruth always remembered that and said it over
And over to herself like a charm or proverb:
Wishing the time away won't make it go.

And so the dress was folded and laid away
A hidden blue all through the long white months.
From time to time Johanna opened the drawer
To touch the dress but not to take it out.

And there were times, when the outer world was white

Or dark, that Edith would come and open the drawer
To rediscover blue.
                    But once, one day,
Her hand in moving among the soft blue folds
Touched something hard and cold, the steel of an ax.
Startled she drew it out. What did it mean?
A feeling stranger than fear was over her.
She hesitated, put it back with the dress,
And closed the drawer.
                        The old year dwindled away
And died with the snow and a new child year was born.
And Eden wrote of little Judd in his bath.
You should see him now. He loves the water so.
He'll be a sailor like his Uncle Leif.

Edith was standing by an open window.
The April air was warm, evocative.
The curtains barely stirred.—And there was Leif
Sauntering down the pasture toward the house,
Leif with his corduroy trowsers and old blue shirt
Open at the throat and the sleeves rolled up,
No cap, and nothing in his hands, and coming.
She ran to the door before there was time to reason.

She looked. She ran out calling softly, Leif,
Leif, to let him know she knew the secret.
She wouldn't tell the others, spoil his surprise.
Leif! He didn't answer. He didn't whistle
Or laugh and step out from behind a tree.
He hadn't heard. He wasn't there.
                                    She stood
And shivered knowing that it would take more heat
Than sun ever to warm her through again.

Sylvester's custom was to bring the mail
Each morning. There was never very much.
Sometimes a letter from Eden, and always the hope
Of one from Leif.
                    The morning when it came
John for the moment was alone in the room.
It was not from Leif. The envelope told that.
It had come from far, had been a long time coming.
John opened his knife to cut the envelope.

He didn't cut it. He laid the letter down
Uncut. It was too heavy for his hand.

Beyond the window a pear tree was in bloom.
Without a wind a petal fluttered, fell.

John picked the letter up and cut it open
And read it, and having read, he folded it
And put it back within the envelope
With the passionless precision of a ghost.

He took the letter out and read it through
Slowly the second time. It fell to the floor.

Why was everything so quiet in the house?
Johanna wondered coming in from her garden.
Nearly noontime. Were they all away?
A sound from the livingroom. She went to the door.

Her father sat in a chair. He did not see her,
Would not have seen her had she spoken his name
Any more than a statue would have turned its stone
Eyes and seen her. He did not even see
Or hear the mother sobbing at his knee,
Hiding her face in her arms.
                              Johanna knew.
Death was the word that no one dared to say.
Death was darkenss and the beautiful deer.
Death was lightning, storm, the sea Leif loved
Drawing him down and down with open eyes.
Nothing in all the world would be the same.
No tree, no bird, no cloud. And they themselves
Would all be strangers.

                    After that first night
When morning came they looked at one another
As wornout travelers might who meet in a desert,
People who do not know each other's language.
How can they speak? They look at one another
Then turn away their eyes.
                          Death was at home
On the hill. They had to take him in, make room.
And he was always taking more and more.

Everything Leif had ever had or touched
Or seen or said or done or wanted to do
Death took. Day after day. Nothing was left.
Even their bodies. Even the food they ate.

They did their work. Sometimes they slept at night.
Sleeping and waking were so much the same,
And days were numbers on the calendar.
Death grew familiar. What was always strange
Was Leif's not being there where he belonged—
Coming indoors or going out of the house,
Out at the barn, off somewhere in the woods,
Asleep in bed. Had been and might have been
Were still too near.
                    Time flowing on flowed back
And Leif was twelve again with his twelve candles
White and burning on the supper table
And he was leaning dark-eyed over the table
Blowing them out, all twelve, with one long breath.

Or he was half that age, a little boy
Maneuvering his ship on the swimming-pool sea,
Alone and happy and no one watching him.

Or when the birthdays were by months not years,
And his only ship was his crib and the sea was sleep.

The hour when night is pregnant with the day
Edith often woke and saw day born.
Sometimes she left her bed. (She seemed a ghost
To herself, was willing to be a ghost that hour.)
And all she ever would do was go to a window
And stand a while.
                    One morning she went farther.
Whiteness of mist and a moon low in the sky.
She dressed and went outdoors and on until
She was above the mist and looking down
And off at green dark islands washed by a sea
Of foam suspended, smoother than any sea.
She shivered. There was no ship. She drew her coat
About her closer and turned to go, but turning
Saw where a knife had onetime cut a name
Bold and deep in a log of the tower, Leif.

By noon the sun had burned the last of the mist
And brought out flowers where none had been before
And dried up puddles and warmed an early snake
Against a stone, but Edith was still cold.
Fire warmed her face. She wore her winter coat.
After she had gone to bed the blankets
Weighed on her but could not make her warm.

That evening Doctor Moor was on the hill.
The two men came from Edith's room together
And faced each other in tacit question and answer.

I'll stay here overnight, the doctor said.

Standing they looked each other in the eye
Aware of other times they had faced each other.

Night came again, and the doctor was still there.
And Edith's room whether by night or day
Was a quiet place except for the sound of breathing.
Johanna went about the house on tiptoe.
Whatever the doctor said to do she did
And did as if she always had known the way.

Once when they happened to be alone together—
How many years ago was it, Johanna,
That summer day when I was here for dinner
And sat across from you, do you remember?
And asked you a question? You wouldn't remember that.
You were a little girl with large blue eyes.
You had been making stories out of your food,
Making believe that food was other things.
I asked you, Does it make the food taste better?
Do you remember? You said Of course it does.
As if I ought to have known. And so I had.
That must have been the year that Leif was twelve.

Nine years ago, she said, and I was seven.

Does that seem very long ago, Johanna?
Seven and nine together seem short to me.
She lay where she lies now, and you were born.
I see those years in you, but not in her.

But can you see ahead? Can you see tomorrow?

Oh, if we could, would we ever dare to look?

But if you have to see you have to see.
Her voice was not as it had been. Her eyes
Were fixed on something not in the room. I see.
I saw Leif drown. And now I see her dying.
We die from what we love. It has to be.

They sat there feeling the creep of time, not moving.
A clock was ticking, and then it told the hour.

VI

Where pasture meets and mingles with the wood
There is a boulder sheltered from the wind
Where one can sit and look out over the world
Through living arabesques of summer leaves
Or winter twigs.
                    They did not move the boulder
Or try to change its shape or carve a name.
Those who were left would not forget the name.

Once this had been Johanna's livingroom
Where she had sat and visited with trees.
The walls were also trees and the ceiling sky
And the floor was earth and grass where insects lived
And where in April pale anemones
Opened their timid petals to the sun.
Edith's flower they were, for her, from her.

And Leif was also there, having come back
As unaccountably as wind or clouds.
All that was left of death was in the house
And in her father's face and voice and silence.

If John had any god it was his ax,
A very active god worshipped in use,
A sharp undeviating god of judgment
Dividing the dead limb from the living tree,
Dividing the dead tree from the living forest.
It cut and split more wood than winter burned

And kept more pasture clear than there was need
Unless the keeping the wide view were need.

But the trees that screened the boulder, small gray birches,
Weeds of trees and worthless except to flutter
Bright green triangles of leaves in May
That turned to yellow in fall—he left untouched.

Gradual growth, gradual decay,
And little else to tell the years apart.
Years had once had shapes of their own like hills
Along the sky, But now they blurred, they merged
In the mist of time.
                              There in that livingroom
The conversation was by insects, birds—
The chickadees and inconspicuous sparrows.
And only rarely, sitting on the stone
And listening, Johanna spoke herself.

Do you remember, Leif? Don't you remember?—
Mother, if you were I, if you were I—

November afternoon was a sky of steel,
Of cloud as cold and smooth and hard a blue
As if it were the ultimate sky, and earth
All brown and gray, all equilibrium.

I'm going out. I'm going over the hill,
Said John. We'll have till supper. So leave your work.
We both stay home too much in an empty house.

They went up through the pasture, the last green places,
Up through the orchard winter-ready and on
To the wood. Their feet were noisy in the leaves
Until they reached the quiet evergreens.
They skirted the peak, pausing neither for breath
Nor view.
            On the farther slope there had been a farm,
An old-stone almost prehistoric place
With stones in the cellar hole and in the well,
Stones that had been a wall, and one a grave.
They stopped as if it were a destination.

They never saw their house a cellar hole,
Johanna said, with trees growing out of it
And people, strangers, sitting on the stones.
They never saw us here.
                    Perhaps, said John,
We see ourselves too clearly and the world
Not clearly enough. Johanna, why do you stay?

Too startled to speak she only stared at him
Not sure she understood.
                    But where would I go,
Father? Then more softly, Why should I go?

He did not look up at her.
                    You're here, she said.
Mother is here. And Leif—
                    Leif is not here.
Girl, your mother is dead. Your brother is dead,
Dead as the people who lived here an age ago.
Ruth and Sylvester are as good as dead.
And I'm not sure but your father is also dead.

Why did you ever come to live on this hill?
She cried standing. Why did you bring them with you,
Mother and Leif and Eden? Why was I born here?
Why have I loved it if I was not to live here
Always, always? Why are you my father
If I am not to love you, if I must leave you?

Still he did not look from the ground to her.
He seemed an old man sitting on a stone.

Father, she whispered, forgive me. Father, father.

He stood slowly. They started home together.

After supper when the dishes were done
And they had sat for a time sharing one lamp
And the silence, John laid down his book in his lap
As if it were too hard to understand.
Hearing his breathing rhythmic and heavier
Johanna looked and saw he was asleep—

An old man, almost, sleeping in his chair.
And she thought of the time when she had been the one
To nod and he had been the one awake.
Time for all little girls to be in bed.
Father, she whispered, but not for him to hear,
Forgive me, forgive me.
                              She was often alone
In the house or near the house most of the day
Most of the time too busy to feel alone.
Dinnertime would come and dinner ready
And he would not be there. She would go to the door
And call and look up toward the wood and listen,
But he would probably be too far to hear.
So she would set the hot food back in the oven
And run up through the pasture to the wood
And the sound of his ax.
                              Father, she would call,
Dinner is ready.
                              Reluctantly he would pause,
Look up and see her, then take another stroke
Or two, or even pretend he had not heard
And go on chopping till she came and stood
Silent as near to him as it was safe,
Until he had to see her. And even then
He would wait until she had started back to the house
Before he started.—The mystery of man
Who loves his dinner but has to be coaxed to come
And eat it. Sylvester had been different.
His little delays had been a luxury
Of anticipation. John's need was forgetting.

She tried to keep him home, not for her sake
And not to save the trees. Through an open doorway
Once she had seen him stoop to pick up something,
Suddenly stop, his hand go to his heart,
Then slowly straighten, stand there staring down.
It was the first time she had seen it happen
Or ever guessed that such a thing might happen.

She did not let him know. Later that day,
Father, will you let me ask you a favor?
I'm lonely when you're away from home so long.
Stay home one day. Stay home tomorrow. Will you,

Father?
          His answer was either answer, silence.

                    .   .   .   .

Between the fall of leaves and the fall of snow
The interregnum, age of bronze and silver.
The last warmth of the year. The winter apples
Picked, the rowan in, the garden ploughed.
The earth grown richer with the summer's leaves.
A quiet time. A time for going to sleep.

Dinner was ready but John had not come in.
Johanna went to the door. She could hear no sound
Of chopping.
          Far away, she thought, or resting
Or maybe starting home.
                    She went to meet him.
Reaching the edge of forest she called to him, Father.

No answer unless the cry of a distant crow
Were answer or the rustle of dead leaves.
The trees stood listening.
                    She hurried on
Until she came to a tree freshly cut down.
Father?
          A flap of wings as a coal-black crow
Loosened itself from the pinnacle of a spruce,
Slipped evilly through the air and out of sight.

There was black on the ground, a man's black coat left lying
And on the ground beside the coat—
                    Father!
The cry was too low. He didn't turn to her.
He didn't move his hand. He hadn't heard.

Before she could run to him or move at all
She heard it coming up through the solid earth,
Pounding, pounding louder and louder the doom
Until Valhalla and all the mountains round it
Thundered. The end. The end.
                    She was kneeling beside him,
Lifting his head, turning his face to see
The eyes that did not see. And having seen

She let the body sink to the earth again.
All that she wanted now was to lie beside him,
Her face against the earth, and never move
From where she lay or ever open her eyes.

From somewhere far away (the only sound
Left in the desolate world) a crow cawed.

Johanna picked the black coat up from the ground
And laid it over her father and stood a moment
Longer, and then with uncontrollable heart
Turned and fled down the long November hill.

The man who had helped John with the hay that summer
Now dug the second grave beside the boulder
And buried him, and afterwards went home.
He would come again whenever Johanna needed.
Almost she thought she wouldn't need him again.
There was little for him to do that she couldn't do
As well, and no one would have to use again
The ax or saw that winter on the hill.
Besides, who lives alone needs no great fire.

Snow was a benediction on the grave,
Saying the final inarticulate word,
The impartial snow that falls on dwellinghouse
And grave and living tree, making them one.

There was little reason now for staying home
In a house whose rooms were empty all day long
Of everything but furniture and echoes,
Whose closets held old clothes owned by the dead.
Under the sky whatever of death there was
Was a different thing from death under a roof.
And all the echoes out of doors were music.

Days when snow was a mirror for every sound
On the hill, Johanna walking through the woods
Paused sometimes, having heard or thought she had,
Was it someone chopping far away through the trees?
Or someone chopping farther away through years?
Or only a woodpecker pecking on hollow wood?

.   .   .

One summer morning midway between two winters,
The air as innocent as the breath of a cow
At pasture and at peace—a knock at the door
And a young man standing there.
                                    I'm Judd, young Judd.
I've wanted to come for a long time, Aunt Johanna.

He spoke as if he knew her, had always known her.
As if, as if there never had been a time
Before he was born and he had never been
The baby she had never held in her arms.
He stood there at the door on a summer morning—
As simply as that—and called her Aunt Johanna,
With never a suspicion in his eyes
That dead years could come back too suddenly.

Come in, she said. And when they had sat down
In the livingroom, she asked for his father and mother.
She looked in his face to find his father and mother.

Wouldn't you like a drink of cold spring water?

He laughed. How did you know I was so thirsty?

She watched his fingers curved around the glass,
And the ripple of his throat in swallowing.
She took the glass and filled it again and brought it.

That's the best water I ever drank in my life
Or hope to drink—
                        (Breeze through the open window
Parted the white curtains for him a moment.)

—Water Mother drank when she was a girl.
They hardly ever come to see you, do they?
They almost seem to be afraid of something.

Afraid? Afraid of what? Afraid of me?
(She was looking straight at him.) There's no one else.

Oh, I don't know. Perhaps they think you're lonely,
Aunt Johanna, up here all alone.
Perhaps they're afraid of, well, of loneliness.

Her eyes were unrelenting. How does it happen,
She said with a tinge of grimness in her tone,
That *you* are not afraid of me?
                                        He flushed.
I don't see anything to be afraid of.

She went to the window, drew aside the curtain.
How could I be lonely here—with them?

The trees? he asked.
                        They went out into the sun
Then entered the indeterminate light of woods
Where birds had finished singing for the day
Except somewhere an occasional ovenbird
Or vireo. And they themselves said little.

Where there were windows upward through the trees
They sometimes caught sight of a giant cloud (or segment
Of cloud) that was also going over the hill—
Almost too great to be a cumulus,
Almost a thunderhead with a hint of darkness.
But it was morning.
                        They came to the place of stones.
Two or three travesties of apple trees
Were still enough alive to be bearing fruit
Crabapple-size. Judd took a bite from one,
Then spit it out, threw the apple away, and laughed.
Sour, he said.
                They sat down on the stones.

It must be a good many years since people lived here.

A small snake sunning itself near blackberry vines
Slid into the cellar hole and disappeared.
The insidious scent of something faintly sweet
Judd didn't know and hardly was aware of—
Sweetbriar.
                I wish Grandfather were still here,
He said. I wish I'd known him, really known him.

He used to sit on the stone you're sitting on,
Johanna said, whenever we rested here.
That was his seat and this was always mine.

A clump of tansy in bloom was growing there
For her to brush her hand against as she talked—
Tansy the strong in life, the strong in death,
The enduring herb whose clean and bitter smell
In tombs can outlast the body and its bones.

I must have been a very little girl
When I first came here. I can't remember a time
I didn't come, with others, then alone.
And always it was this ancient sort of place.
We used to wonder who had used to live here.
We never knew their name.
                              The sun was high.
Time to be starting back. Yet they didn't go
For a while. Johanna didn't want to move.
Why should a half hour's walk have made her tired?
She wondered.
                    That night she lay awake while Judd
Slept in the little room that had been Leif's.
No one had slept there after Leif had gone.
So many years of nights the bed had been empty,
And now one night—
                        The glass above her bureau
Had answered only easy questions morning
And evening about her hair, her dress. But now
She was asking more and the glass was slow to answer.
Who was this woman with the tired look?
The gray look though the hair had not yet turned?
Why was she tired? Was it one sleepless night?
Or had she been as tired yesterday?
Too many yesterdays?
                          She looked until
Familiar was unfamiliar. Was this herself?
Or fate? And what was fate if not herself?

When Judd had left and Johanna had made the bed
And was coming out and about to close the door
Again, she stopped. It could stand open now
And if that door, her father's room as well.
The fear had gone. Soon she was going in
And out for other reasons than to dust.
She even brought her sewing at times and sewed there.
Or standing before his books she would take them down

From the shelves, one at a time, and open them
To where his name was written sharp and clean,
And turn the pages till she came to a sentence
Underlined. What had it meant to him?

She opened drawers for the first time in the desk.
She found in one a small black-covered notebook,
Her father's diary of facts, dates,
Condensations, irreducibles,
Each fact as sparely stated as an inscription,
And yet in every word his hand, his voice.
Was it for her to read? What would he wish?
And if she had the right, had she the courage?
So small, so light a book to hold the weight
Of his life. So easily the pages turned,
The years.
              The date: A daughter born, Johanna.

The naked statement. More than statement, fiat.
She read it without breathing. She saw her father
Sitting at his desk writing the words.
She saw him by the bedside looking down
As he must have done at her as she must have been.
And she was looking down through all the years
At herself. All that she had ever known
Or dreamed was after this and out of this.
The book fell closed, forgotten, in her hands.

She saw them coming, and why. His need for a world
Clean-cut, uncompromising, self-contained.
A world of silences and distances.
She saw them building Valhalla of stones and trees
And of themselves. She saw them living there
The years that once seemed many and now seemed few.
All that had happened, even her standing there
In her father's room on a certain day and hour
Was part and had to be.
                        But if she turned,
Now while the past lay open like the landscape,
And looked through the other window would she see
Through time the other way, the flower's fruit?

Young Judd was picking the little apple again,

Taking a bite, spitting it out with a laugh.

That was a thing could always happen—a hand
That suddenly reached and picked and threw away.
But likelier the apple would never be picked,
Would shrivel on the tree until its skin
Was puckered like the face of an old woman.

But was it really sour, the little apple?
Or sweetness sharpened by its opposite?

So many times she asked herself the question.
It wouldn't stay answered. She wanted to tell her father
His flower had not been barren after all,
Or the fruit unpalatable. And yet, and yet—

.   .   .

It was spring when Johanna faced the young physician,
For Doctor Moor was dead and the oracles
Would have to be spoken by someone else, a stranger.

He said: Since you live alone and there is no one,
You say, to care for you, I must tell you the truth.

As a child I was taught to hear and speak the truth,
She answered. Truth has always seemed to me
The least that one could say or listen to.

And then he told her.
                I might have guessed, she murmured.

He spoke of treatment, but she showed no interest.
He told her how long she might expect to live
If nothing were done for her.
                And how much longer,
She asked, if something, if everything, were done?

He stated a maximum and a minimum.

And I would leave my home where I was born
And where I have always lived till now (her tone
Was musing, reminiscence, rather than question)
Knowing that I should never come back to live,

For the sake of a few more months, an extra year
Or two of something neither life nor death
In a hospital?
                    You have that to decide, he said.

She wanted to tell him there were other choices
Than those he had named, that he couldn't pin her down
To A or B or any death by prescription.
She wanted to tell him there was another choice.

Sooner or later, he reminded her,
Of course you—
                    Yes, she answered, Sooner or later.

Hard as a little stone that one might hide
In the hand, yet be detached, not part of the hand,
Hard and small and jewel-clear and secret,
Not to be shown to anyone—the thought
Johanna carried back to the hill and kept
Through day and night. It was always there in her mind,
Like something that could be taken out of a case,
Examined and put back—the other choice.

And so it was till sometime deep in summer
Not all at once, one day, but gradually,
She became aware the thing was part of herself,
Decided. And what she had only thought to do
Was now the thing that sometime would be done.

A stir of coolness on a stifling day.
She began to breathe again. There was air, there was room.
The coming of wind, of storm, and after storm
Clear days, cool nights for sleep, another season.
And clear as the sky and hills could ever be,
Clear as the past and part of the past, the future.

Time that had been the tyrant became her slave.
She told him when to come, to wait, to go.
And every day was a gift she took from him
And gave to herself. Each day a different gift
And each more precious than the one before.

The brilliant days, bluebird and oriole
And dragonfly. Days of the fabulous clouds,
Deep shadows and kaleidoscopic hills.
Windy days and days when the only sound
The wings of an insect somewhere in the air.
Days of the soft and delicate blues, blurred days.
And days of rain in silverpoint or pencil.

One after one Johanna watched them go.
Standing in the pasture or near the wood
And quiet as a tree herself she waited
Until the brightness went from cloud to moon
And her feet were wet with dew.
                              Having come in
At last and closed the door and lighted her lamp,
Sometimes she would go back for an afterlook.

The moon might be down or hidden now, no stars,
And off to the south a trace of thunderhead
Outlined and lit with sudden fire faintly.
That was a thing she might never see again,
Heat lightning and fireflies lighting the night between them.

And there were other, stranger things she saw
Or came near seeing. Shadows passing the window.
(If she had turned her head a moment sooner.)
And sounds—could it be footsteps at the door?

She listened for the knock. Had he come back
Another summer to call her Aunt Johanna,
And drink again cold water from the spring
His mother used to drink from as a girl?
That moment listening for the knock, the voice,
Johanna knew from another nearer sound
How much she hoped he would come and feared he would come.

But there was no knock. She went to the door and stood there
Waiting. Perhaps there had been no sound at all
And what she had seen had only been a bird
Fly past the window. It could have been a bird,

Something with wings, a dragonfly, a moth,
A leaf falling. Or could it, could it have been—

The blackberries and summer apples ripened.
Summer sprawled in the sun, grew fat, and dozed,
And took his time. There were plenty of days ahead,
Plenty of heat to turn the grapes from green
To purple, and bring the flowers that hadn't bloomed.
The weeds grew tall. They had never heard of frost.
And yet to Johanna it was already autumn.
Sunlight was different and the sky at sunset,
Evenings earlier and the incessant insects,
And the wood pewee singing at noon in the shade.
Each year it had always been the same—two tides
That flowed together—autumn the undertide
To summer. Every year she had found it early
And followed it to the fall of leaves and after.

.   .   .

Twelve white candles on the supper table
Burning as calmly as twelve other candles
Once had burned. Johanna sat alone.
Whatever feast it was was not of food.
She ate as one would eat of the Holy Supper.
And when she had finished and sat a little longer
Watching the candles, she stood and blew them out.

The time had come, the day. There had been frost
To turn the maples along the edge of the pasture
And there would be frost again on the hill tonight.
If stars were proof, the morning would be clear,
And what she had to do required clearness.

Night by night she had sat by the open fire
Reading old letters, burning those she had read.
And lastly she had burned the small black book,
Her father's. Fire the uncompromising, the final.

And so the morning. Having bathed and dressed,
Having brushed and carefully arranged her hair,
She went to her desk. She had two letters to write,
Not long. There was little she needed to say to Eden,

And less to the man who would be coming soon
To cut and bring in wood. Dear Sister Eden—

She went from room to room to look once more
From windows, and as she passed she paused to touch
A book, picture, bed.
                Outdoors the mist
Was clearing and the fire of maples and sumachs
And blueberry bushes was burning through. This
Was the fire that long ago had been in her mind
When they had told her of the great Valhalla.

Taking a certain intricate little tool
Her father had taught her long ago to use,
She went up through the pasture to the place
Where the others were. The sky was blue perfection
Washed and new. No wind, no thought of wind.
Shadows on the ground were white, but frost
Was dew in the sun.
              She stood beside the boulder,
Touching it with her hand to feel again
The lastingness, the immovability.
Through yellow leaves of birch (a few leaves falling)
The blue of hills.
           This was obedience,
Not to her father's word or anything
He ever dreamed would come, but to his life.
The clean sharp end as he himself would have it.

She looked down at the shining tool in her hand.
A fly, warmed by the sun to flying, lit
On the steel. She studied the iridescent wings,
The delicate feet. There was time enough for that.
She thought of all the life on the hill, the insects.
What was one life against their countless lives?
And the birds, they would always be coming back each spring.
And trees, the trees would be there.
             The fly had vanished.
Her going would be a little thing like that.

She lifted her hand and as she did she saw
The deer's dark eyes, the storm, the lightning, Audhumbla.

She pressed the thing against her heart and fired.

Angry, a crow dislodged itself from a tree
And flew away. A thin blue dragonfly
On a stem of grass had darted, circled, returned.
Over the ground the ants kept on with their business
Undisturbed. The air moved just enough
To take another leaf, and then was still.

1944

The Sound I Listened For

The Sound I Listened For

What I remember is the ebb and flow of sound
That summer morning as the mower came and went
And came again, crescendo and diminuendo,
And always when the sound was loudest how it ceased
A moment while he backed the horses for the turn,
The rapid clatter giving place to the slow click
And the mower's voice. That was the sound I listened for.
The voice did what the horses did. It shared the action
As sympathetic magic does or incantation.
The voice hauled and the horses hauled. The strength of one
Was in the other and in the strength was no impatience.
Over and over as the mower made his rounds
I heard his voice and only once or twice he backed
And turned and went ahead and spoke no word at all.

Juniper

From where I live, from windows on four sides
I see four common kinds of evergreen:
White pine, pitch pine, cedar, and juniper.
The last is less than tree. It hugs the ground.
It would be last for any wind to break
If wind could break the others. Pines would go first
As some of them have gone, and cedars next,
Though where is wind to blow a cedar down?
To overthrow a juniper a wind
Would have to blow the ground away beneath it.

125

Not wind but fire. I heard a farmer say
One lighted match dropped on a juniper
Would do the trick. And he had done the trick.
I try to picture how it would look: thin snow
Over the pasture and dark junipers
Over the snow and darker for the snow,
Each juniper swirl-shaped like flame itself.
Then from the slow green fire the swift hot fire
Flares, sputters with resin, roars, dies
While the next juniper goes next.

                              Poets
Are rich in points of view if they are rich
In anything. The farmer thinks one thing;
The poet can afford to think all things
Including what the farmer thinks, thinking
Around the farmer rather than above him,
Loving the evergreen the farmer hates,
And yet not hating him for hating it.

I know another fire in juniper,
Have felt its heat burn on my back, have breathed
Its invisible smoke, climbing New England hills
In summer. Have known the concentrated sun
Of hard blue berries, chewed them, and spit them out,
Their juice burning my throat. Juniper.

Its colors are the metals: tarnished bronze
And copper, violet of tarnished silver,
And if you turn it, white aluminum.
So many colors in so dull a green
And I so many years before I saw them.

I see those colors now, and far, far more
Than color. I see all that we have in common
Here where we live together on this hill.
And what I hope for is for more in common.

Here is my faith, my vision, my burning bush.
It will burn on and never be consumed.
It will be here long after I have gone,
Long after the last farmer sleeps. And since
I speak for it, its silence speaks for me.

The Old of the Moon in August

"The old of the moon in August," the old man said,
"Is the time to cut your brush. You cut it then
You won't be having to cut it off again."

I judge he meant the dead that month stay dead.
I must remember—August, the August moon,
The old of the moon, the old of the moon. Amen.

As Near to Eden

Hearing the cry I looked to see a bird
Among the boughs that overhung the stream.
No bird was there. The cry was not a bird's.
Then I looked down and saw the snake and saw
The frog. Half of the frog was free to cry.
The other half the snake had in its jaws.
The snake was silent as the sand it lay on.

I ran to blast the thing out of my sight,
But the snake ran first (untouched) into the water
Fluid to fluid and so disappeared
And all I saw and heard was flowing water.

I dipped a foot in slowly and began
To saunter down the stream a little way
As I had done so many times before
That summer. Now I went more cautiously
Watching the water every step, but water
Had washed the thing away and washed it clean.

Over the stream I had a kind of bed
Built of an old smooth board and four large stones
And there between the sun and water I
Would often spend an early afternoon.
It was as near to Eden as I knew—

This altenating cool and warm, this blend
Of cool and warm, of water-song and silence.
No one could see me there and even insects
Left me alone.
                        I turned upon my face
And so had darkness for my eyes and fire
On my back. I felt my breathing slacken, deepen.
After a time I reached a hand over
And let the fingertips trail in the water.

Strange, strange that in a world so old and rich
In good and evil, the death (or all but death)
Of one inconsequential squealing frog
Should have concerned me so, should for the moment
Have seemed the only evil in the world
And overcoming it the only good.

But they were symbols too, weren't they? the frog,
The snake? The frog of course being innocence
Sitting with golden and unwinking eyes
Hour after hour beside a water-weed
As rapt and meditative as a saint
Beneath a palm tree, and the snake being—well,
That's all been told before.
                        A pretty contrast,
Yet even under the indulgent sun
And half asleep I knew my picture false.
The frog was no more innocent than the snake
And if he looked the saint he was a fake.
He and the snake were all too closely kin,
First cousins once removed under the skin.
If snakes ate frogs, frogs in their turn ate flies
And both could look ridiculously wise.
But neither one knew how to feed on lies
As man could do; that is, philosophize.
And having reached that point I closed my eyes,
Rhyming myself and sunning myself to sleep.

And while I slept my body was a sundial
Casting its moving, slowly moving shadow
Across the moving, swiftly moving water.

When I awoke I had one clear desire:
The coolness of that swiftly moving water.
Yet still I waited, it was so near, so sure,
The superfluity of heat so good.

And then I sat straight up having heard a sound
I recognized too well. It was no bird.
Slipping and splashing as I went I ran
Upstream. I couldn't see, I didn't need
To see to know. So all the time I'd slept
And sunned myself and entertained myself
With symbolizing and unsymbolizing
Good and evil, *this* had been going on.

They were hidden now among the roots of a tree
The stream had washed the soil from. I found a stick
And jabbed it in as far as I could reach
Again and again until I broke the stick.
But still I kept it up until the snake
Having disgorged slipped out and got away.
And still I kept it up until the frog
Must have been pulp and ground into the sand.
The stick, all that was left, I threw as far
As I could throw.
                      Then I went home and dressed.
Eden was done for for one day at least.

That Dark Other Mountain

My father could go down a mountain faster than I
Though I was first one up.
Legs braced or with quick steps he slid the gravel slopes
Where I picked cautious footholds.

Black; Iron, Eagle, Doublehead, Chocorua,
Wildcat and Carter Dome—
He beat me down them all. And that last other mountain.
And that dark other mountain.

Altitude

We heard their cries before we saw the crows,
A score of them. But one is not a crow.
The shape is longer, sharper-winged—a hawk.

Coolly he circles round and round, dodging
Their beaks, enduring those he cannot dodge.
But all the while he wheels he also rises

Slowly, so slowly we can't see him rise.
We see that he is higher than he was.
We hear the anger of the crows come fainter.

At last one crow drops off and then another.
Then five or six are straggling down the sky.
Then only two are left. Then one. Then none.

The hawk is now a fly on a blue wall.
Nothing is near him. He is high enough.
He takes his time, drifting away to west.

The Laughers

I drove an old man to a funeral
And on the way he said, "What do they mean,
These men who die at sixty, sixty-five?
Here I am going on to seventy-two
And hard at work. Of course my heart is bad
And I have kidney stones, but otherwise—"

I told my father and he laughed. He laughed
Less than two years ago and I laughed with him.
Now both of them—the laugher and the man
We laughed about—have gone to where nobody
(This is a joke my father would enjoy)
Laughs, or if he does, nobody hears.

Perspective

It just occurs to me, here in the sun,
Warming my back in winter-morning sun,
That after the war is ended and all the dead
Have died, I might be one to go on living.
It just occurs to me I might be one.

I might (it would be possible) grow old,
Finish my work with time left over, time
For remembering. It might, it could be so.
An old man watching vegetables grow,
Hoeing his beans or resting on his hoe.

And would some youngster ask the old man questions?
Some boy so tuned-and-tingling to his world,
So clear, so unacquainted with confusion
The sight of him could fool you into thinking
That evil was some old absurd delusion?

What would he say, the old man as he pauses
Over his rows of beans? What would he say
Of heroes who had or hadn't had their day,
Of martyrs, scoundrels, and ordinary men,
Of oceans, continents, and historic causes?

But if the boy should ask, But you were there?
The old man takes his hoe and starts to work.
I couldn't hear whatever it was he said.
The sun floods in. I shield from the glare
To read the estimates of the past day's dead.

Three Woodchoppers

Three woodchoppers walk up the road.
Day after day it is the same.
The short man always takes the lead
Limping like one a trifle lame.

131

And number two leans as he goes
And number three walks very straight.
I do not time them but I know
They're never early, never late.

So I have seen them for a week,
Have seen them but have heard no sound.
I never saw one turn to speak.
I never saw one look around.

Out of a window to the south
I watch them come against the light.
I cross the room and to the north
I watch till they are out of sight.

Winter

The wasp upon the windowpane
Observes the brief day wax and wane.

The year is old.
The glass is cold.

How should he whirr electric wings
Who cannot crawl, who only clings?

How should he fly
Who cannot try?

The strength is there but not the will.
The nerves are stung. The brain is still.

Afternoon Drive

Decorously at half-past four
As winter dusk begins to fall
A long black car rolls up next door
To make a tea-time Sunday call.

I see it but I hear no sound
For there is smooth December snow
Over the hard December ground.
And now the headlights are turned low.

For men go up and ring the bell
And then they disappear inside.
I think (though one can never tell)
They've come to take someone to ride.

And if they have, I think I know
Who's going for a breath of air.
She never used to like the snow,
But now I think she doesn't care.

And here they come and they are five
And all of them are wearing black.
And there they go to take their drive
But only four are coming back.

The Goldfish Bowl

The year is nineteen forty-one, the season winter.
The earth lies naked to the wind. The frost goes deep.
Along the river shore the ice-sheets creak and splinter.
Under the frost the tree roots and the woodchuck sleep.

The time is winter night, but in the swimming pool
Is summer noontime, noon by the electric sun.
The young men dive, emerge, and float a while, and fool,
And dive again. The year is nineteen forty-one.

The tropic water is safe-filtered and the room
Is air-conditioned, kept an even eighty-five.
Outdoors a shivering newsboy is proclaiming doom.
Inside the pool a naked youth is poised to dive.

The time is ten o'clock in nineteen forty-one.
Somewhere a bell upon a tower begins to toll,
While hour by hour the moon, its fat face warm with sun,
Gloats like a patient cat above a goldfish bowl.

133

Indoor Lady

An indoor lady whom I know
Laments the lateness of the spring—
The sun, the birds, the buds so slow,
The superannuated snow,
The wind that is possessed to blow.

Her sadly window-watching eyes,
Her uttered and unuttered sighs,
For such unseasonable skies
Give me to understand that spring
In other years was otherwise.

The Thief

Now night the sneak thief comes
Warily from the woods,
Shadowing our homes,
Greedy for all our goods.

Doors cannot keep him out.
Windows are for his peeping.
Soon he will roam about
In rooms where we are sleeping.

Who knows what he will take?
What he will leave behind?
Who knows when we awake
What we shall never find?

The Mouse Whose Name Is Time

The Mouse whose name is Time
Is out of sound and sight.
He nibbles at the day
And nibbles at the night.

He nibbles at the summer
Till all of it is gone.
He nibbles at the seashore.
He nibbles at the moon.

Yet no man not a seer,
No woman not a sibyl
Can ever ever hear
Or see him nibble, nibble.

And whence or how he comes
And how or where he goes
Nobody dead remembers,
Nobody living knows.

Good Night Near Christmas

And now good night. Good night to this old house
Whose breathing fires are banked for their night's rest.
Good night to lighted windows in the west.
Good night to neighbors and to neighbors' cows

Whose morning milk will be beside my door.
Good night to one star shining in. Good night
To earth, poor earth with its uncertain light,
Our little wandering planet still at war.

Good night to one unstarved and gnawing mouse
Between the inner and the outer wall.
He has a paper nest in which to crawl.
Good night to men who have no bed, no house.

Five Silver Foxes

Her velvet cape is trimmed with five
Silver foxes (so runs the cable).
Only the lady is alive,
The sole survivor of the fable.

Five silver foxes set the fashion,
So soft, so lustrous, so expensive.
For fox fur she confessed a passion.
But is the lady apprehensive?

Five silver foxes in a row
And one fox hides the crucifix.
How does the silver lady know
That she will not be number six?

Old Man Feeding Hens

The oldest-looking man, the slowest-moving,
I ever saw, dressed all in somber black
And with a great December-snowdrift beard,
Leans on a staff and with his other hand
Feeds a few Barred-Rock hens from a slung basket.

Neither the man nor hens make any sound
For me to overhear. One might suppose
That he had passed beyond the need of words,
Either to speak them or to hear them spoken,
And that his hens had grown into his silence.

The house beside him is a Barred-Rock gray
With not one window-sign of habitation.
Some day and soon it will have less than none,
And on that day the hens may not be fed
Till noon or evening or the second morning.

Willow Woman

A woman with pinched fingers and pinched face
Is selling pussy-willows on the street.
The buds are wearing something fine in fur.
A burlap rag is rug about her feet.

Nobody buys. Nobody stops for her.
Poor woman, willow woman, don't you know
It's only winter in the marketplace
However springlike where the willows grow?

It May Not Comfort You

It may not comfort you to know—
But if the time should ever come
When lily and delphinium
Are trampled to their doom
And only weeds are left to grow—

(Where has the gardener gone?
And who will mow the lawn?)

It may be comfort in your need
To find the goldenrod in bloom,
To find it flower and not weed.

If We Had Known

If we had known all that we know
We never would have let him go.

He never would have reached the river
If we had guessed his going. Never.

We had the stronger argument
Had we but dreamed his dark intent.

Or if our words failed to dissuade him
Unarguing love might still have stayed him.

We would have lured him from his course.
And if love failed, there still was force.

We would have locked the door and barred it.
We would have stood all night to guard it.

But what we know, we did not know.
We said good-bye and saw him go.

Socrates and the Crowd

Socrates could ponder in a crowd
As you or I might ponder in a wood,
Whether he pondered silent or aloud,
The crowd might bump against him: there he stood.

Stood like a tree and no man could disturb him
No more than we would be disturbed by trees.
And when he moved to talk no man could curb him.
And how he loved to talk—this Socrates.

They were amused until they were offended.
They got him down.—Now where were you and I
That day they thought the incident was ended
And Socrates at last took time to die?

Serpent as Vine

Once I observed a serpent climb a tree.
Just once. It went up twisting like a vine,
Around, around, then out across a branch,
And though it went up faster than a vine,
It did not seem to hurry as it went.

And having reached a certain bough, it lay
As quiet as a vine. I could not tell
Its secret there among the summer leaves.
But what I knew I knew exceeding well:
That something underfoot was overhead.

I Am Not Flattered

I am not flattered that a bell
About the neck of a peaceful cow
Should be more damning to my ear
Than all the bombing planes of hell
Merely because the bell is near,
Merely because the bell is now,
The bombs too far away to hear.

Spicebush and Witch-Hazel

Spicebush almost the first dark twig to flower
In April woods, witch-hazel last of all—
Six months from flower of spring to flower of fall—
The alpha and omega if you please.
Yet how alike in color, setting, form:
Both blossoms yellow to confirm the sun,
Both borne on bushes that are nearly trees,
Both close to twig though not to keep them warm.
Only the learned might elucidate
Why one blooms early and one blooms so late.
Only the wise could tell the wiser one.

The Wasp

As I was reading, a wasp lit on the page
Whose burden was that man knows nothing, nothing,
And slowly walked across. And at the edge

It paused to reconsider. I paused too.
I took it for a marginal annotation.
I let the text go and I read the wasp.

Or rather say, I tried to read the wasp.
I turned the book this way and that the way
A child might try a Greek word upside-down.

139

I counted feelers, wings, and legs, for letters.
I looked it in the eye but could not tell
Whether for certain it returned my look.

Perhaps the gist of what the side-note said
Was that a wasp could read the printed word
As well as man could read the total world.

Or else the meaning may have been that man,
If he knows nothing, knows that he knows nothing,
Whereas the wasp knows only what it knows.

Shadows

One of the shadows in my boyhood mind
Made me avoid night shadows on the ground—
Shadows of telephone poles, shadows of trees.
I would not step on one if I could help it.
I leaped them like a runner leaping hurdles.

The fear (if it was strong enough to call
A fear) was not the shadow but the touch,
Though what the consequence of touching was
I never knew, I never even asked.

How many nights ago that was. Tonight
The shadows that I fear (if fear it is)
Are not tree shadows crisscrossing the road
Or any shadows I could ever leap.

Where Is the Island?

The talk was difficult and deep and long:
Peace in a warring world. During a pause
A child they had forgotten in the room
Asked, Couldn't all the people who love peace
Live on an island far away at sea?

So innocent-wise it was they scarcely smiled.
An old man answered gently, Where is the island
Large enough, my child, to hold us all?
And were we but a handful, where is the island
Small enough and bare enough and far
Enough away that hunters wouldn't come
With dogs and guns and hunt us like wild geese?

You don't mean wild geese, do you? said the child.
Only the dogs and hunters would be wild.

Poverty Grass

Beyond the tenements of the town,
Beyond the tin-roofed hoi polloi,
The railroad and the highway pass
Field after field of poverty grass
Which, heaven knows, is rich enough
In every hue from red to brown,
And when it feathers out with fluff
Matches a tow-haired sunburned boy.

From end of summer on into winter
It undulates as the wind blows it.
Brighter than loam, darker than flame,
Only age can make it fainter.
Only deep snow can subdue it.
Of all the passersby that view it
Rare is the passerby that knows it
Or knows the irony of its name.

April Thunder

I was awake enough to wonder
And certainly awake to hear it—
That single clap of April thunder.

141

It sounded like a threat of danger.
It sounded very much like anger
Only more remote and stranger.

Whether or not it was a warning
It broke the stillness of the long winter
And the brief stillness of the morning.

Boy Sleeping

Don't wake him. Let him sleep a little longer.
Give him another hour. Breakfast will keep.
He will be hungry but for now his hunger
And food are less to him than bed and sleep.

Waking can be almost as slow as birth is—
A boy his age—and Sunday morning. Let
Him be slow and sleep, as slow as April earth is,
And after all he's only April yet.

Interrupted Fern

Interrupted fern we call it
As if design for reproduction
Were nothing but an imperfection.
As if we disapproved the function.
As if of all the ferns and bracken
This were faulty and mistaken.
As if the fern called for correction—
The fern and not our empty fiction,
The fern and not our clumsy diction.
Henceforth I take this fern as token
Of all things fertile, whole, unbroken.

Answer

The age is fourteen and the hour of morning three.
My flashlight for a moment plays the moon on him
Lying as sleeping water lies beneath the moon,
His only motion breathing

I have come in to draw a blanket over him.
The night turns cooler after storm. I hear the stir
Of leaves beyond the window, see the sky with stars.
Tomorrow will be clear.

Remembering blunders, I can find no blunder now,
No slamming door or door left open for the flies,
No fumbled or unfinished thing, no trace of flaw,
But only perfect sleep

Feeling the blanket's warmth, he sighs a sleeper's sigh
That says enough although it says but little. So
My flashlight lights me back to bed, my questions answered,
Such as have an answer.

Old Roofs

Old roofs that only yesterday
Were dingy indiscriminate gray

With no appreciable design
And not one clean-cut slope or line

Now startle and delight the eye—
Clear white against the winter sky.

Their surfaces are all intact,
Their corners sharp, their lines exact

As if their purpose was to show
The plane geometry of snow.

They look like problems waiting proof—
Your roof, my roof, any old roof.

143

Salt

Salt for white
And salt for pure.
What's salted right
Will keep and cure.

Salt for cheap
And salt for free.
The poor may reap
Salt from the sea.

Salt for taste
And salt for wit.
Be wise. Don't waste
A pinch of it.

Sing a Song of Juniper

Sing a song of juniper
Whose song is seldom sung,
Whose needles prick the finger,
Whose berries burn the tongue.

Sing a song of juniper
With boughs shaped like a bowl
For holding sun or snowfall
High on the pasture knoll.

Sing a song of juniper
Whose green is more than green,
Is blue and bronze and violet
And colors in between.

Sing a song of juniper
That keeps close to the ground,
A song composed of silence
And very little sound.

Sing a song of juniper
That hides the hunted mouse,
And gives me outdoor shadows
To haunt my indoor house.

Incident

A boy of maybe nine or ten
Got up quietly from his place
And came and kissed us all good night,
The women first and then the men.
We saw he wasn't very bright,
Yet there was starlight on his face.

Light against Light

When thunder woke him in the night and shades
Drawn down could not hide lightning from his eyes,
Instead of trying to hide it from his eyes
She gave him magic lightning of his own
With power to use it any time he willed.

So every time the outer lightning flashed,
A small boy in an upstairs room alone
Flashed back at it. As men fight fire with fire
So he fought light with light. And when at last
He slept, he held the flashlight in his hand.

Sight

I might see more if I were blind—
The sightless eyes, the illumined mind.
I might find what I've failed to find.

Sight can be a foe to sight.
Darkness can be friend to light
Even as stars are friends of night.

White Sunday Morning

White Sunday morning long ago—
White bedroom curtains and white walls,
Beyond the window falling snow
That dillydallies as it falls,
And in the kitchen down below
An old old woman popping corn,
Popping corn on Sunday morning.
Thanks to the little register
Cut in my floor above her stove
I can look down and spy on her
And overhear her every move.
And every move she makes is slow,
Pushing the popper to and fro.
I hear the corn begin to pop.
O sing, white church, that Christ is born.
I do not hear your singing choir,
I only hear the popping corn
Until I hear the popping stop.
But now, praise be, I more than hear it,
For lifted on the breath of fire
The fragrance rises like pure spirit.
The fragrance rises while the snow
Is falling, falling long ago.

Now That Your Shoulders Reach My Shoulders

My shoulders once were yours for riding.
My feet were yours for walking, wading.
My morning once was yours for taking.

Still I can almost feel the pressure
Of your warm hands clasping my forehead
While my hands grasped your willing ankles.

Now that your shoulders reach my shoulders
What is there left for me to give you?
Where is a weight to lift as welcome?

The Hay Is Cut

The hay is cut, the field is clean
And smooth as (seen from here) a lawn.
The sky is clear and tinged with green.
The men have come and hayed and gone.

The hay is in, the men are home.
Against the sky a hill looms tall.
Three months of summer still must come
And yet to me tonight is fall.

Young Farmer

One glance at him and you can tell
His fruit is clean, his corn is tall.
His sheep and cattle pastured well,
His buildings trim: house, barn, and wall.

You know the seed he sows is sound
As seed his forefathers have sown.
And when he ploughs and plants the ground
The crop must grow as he has grown.

Excellence

Excellence is millimeters and not miles.
From poor to good is great. From good to best is small.
From almost best to best sometimes not measurable.
The man who leaps the highest leaps perhaps an inch
Above the runner-up. How glorious that inch
And that split-second longer in the air before the fall.

Who Comes as Light

Who comes as light
Need never wait outside.
Who brings the day
Always has right of way
To enter here,
Has leave to pass
Instant as light through glass.
Who comes as light
Will find these windows wide,
The glass washed clear.

Coming and Going

The crows are cawing,
The cocks are crowing,
The roads are thawing,
The boys are bumming,
The winds are blowing,
The year is coming.

The jays are jawing,
The cows are lowing,
The trees are turning,
The saws are sawing,
The fires are burning,
The year is going.

Summons

Keep me from going to sleep too soon
Or if I go to sleep too soon
Come wake me up. Come any hour
Of night. Come whistling up the road.
Stomp on the porch. Bang on the door.
Make me get out of bed and come
And let you in and light a light.
Tell me the northern lights are on
And make me look. Or tell me clouds
Are doing something to the moon
They never did before, and show me.
See that I see. Talk to me till
I'm half as wide awake as you
And start to dress wondering why
I ever went to bed at all.
Tell me the walking is superb.
Not only tell me but persuade me.
You know I'm not too hard persuaded.

Fruit

If poems ever dropped into my hand,
If there was ever any time
In any land
When I had but to shake the bough
For the ripe fruit to fall,
It is not so now.

Today the fruit I want is fruit I pick.
I have to climb,
I have to reach,
I have to be both slow and quick
For each particular blue plum
Or golden peach.

Bluejays

Always I hear the bluejays
These early autumn blue days,
Taunting the leaves to hurry,
Wanting the snow to flurry,
Wanting a blue-white weather
To match their blue-white feather.
All right, all right, I'm willing
And far far more than willing,
But leave me a few days longer
To satisfy my hunger
For something almost summer
After the end of summer,
When the quiet mind goes gleaning
For odds and ends of meaning
Before the year's transition,
Before the mind's submission.
Then let the jays come screaming
And jar me from my dreaming.

Evening Ride

The world lay still and clear like a long mural
And we who watched were all that moved and we
Could overlook that we ourselves were moving.

There was no wind to flaw the level sunlight
And the long shadows lying on the hills
And chimney smoke pale blue on deep blue air.

Three children by the roadside stopped their play
To gaze. A woman sewing on her porch
Paused with the lifted needle in her hand.

Two farmers with a load of hay half loaded
Stood with their pitchforks idle as we passed.
Even a dog looked and forgot to bark.

The road was always upward. Now it was day,
Now twilight, and now day again. Now warm,
Now cool. We felt the cool grow ever cooler.

Woodsmoke was in the air, late supper cooking,
Fragrance of newmown hay and ancient woods
And evening vines in sudden deep ravines.

We reached the summit but only after the sun
Had gone. The road beyond dipped down to darkness
While higher hills on either hand were bright.

Nothing Is Far

Though I have never caught the word
Of God from any calling bird,
I hear all that the ancients heard.

Though I have seen no deity
Enter or leave a twilit tree,
I see all that the seers see.

A common stone can still reveal
Something not stone, not seen, yet real.
What may a common stone conceal?

Nothing is far that once was near.
Nothing is hid that once was clear.
Nothing was God that is not here.

Here is the bird, the tree, the stone.
Here in the sun I sit alone
Between the known and the unknown.

The Reading of the Psalm

An old woman by a window watching the storm—
Dark river and dark sky and furious wind
Full of green flying leaves, gray flying rain.

Daughters and grandchildren in a darkened room
(The shutters closed, the shades drawn down)
Call to her to come, to come away.

Above the wind and the crash of a porch chair
And now the thunder, she does not seem to hear
Or if she hears, she does not answer them.

At the approach of storm she came upstairs
And closed her bedroom window. She stands there still,
Her hand resting upon the windowsill.

With eyes as calm, as unreproving, gentle
As though she watched the lighting of a candle
She watches how the lightning parts the sky.

Would she be safer were she not alone?
Would she be safer if the shades were drawn?
She does not ask. She does not think of safety.

Rather she thinks of deep roots drinking rain,
Of all dust washed from leaves, of pools filled,
Of cooler air and a good night for sleeping.

And if the lightning (while she stands there watching)
Touched her and closed her eyes— They are calling her
From the darkened room, "Mother, Grandmother, come!"

Slowly she turns away, having heard them call.
Turns from the storm as one might read a psalm
And look away and slowly close the book.

The Four

Two men who never met, two men whose minds
Could not have met except to disagree,
Now for some forty years despite themselves
Have met in me—not in complete accord,
Yet not without some mutual understanding.

One was a craftsman, patienter with wood
Than with his fellow men. A silent man
Who worked alone, and when he couldn't work
Sat lonely in a room with other people.
A man too early old, too soon gone-by,
Passing from house to house, from married daughter
To daughter, playing his games of solitaire
Or prophesying civil war again
Or gazing at the goldfish in their bowl.

The other was a country doctor. If
His photograph is proof, his jaw was law,
His temper was an August thunderstorm.
He was a Nova Scotian Irishman.
He had ten sons and two or three of them
Were documentary evidence their father
Possessed both motherwit and fatherwit.
He died at fifty-seven.
                                How should two men
Who might have found one room too small for them
Now meet together in one mind in peace?

The answer is: there are two others here
Whose names are Patience and Serenity—
My grandmothers. They do not often speak,
They do not need to speak to understand.

Clairvoyance

Remember the day, the summer afternoon
We stood among the trees by the little house
And glancing in, saw we were glancing through
—Window and window—to other trees beyond
As if the house were only a picture frame?

The world was only a picture frame to us
That day—windows with sunlight on both sides.
Was it a tinge of autumn in the air
That made the seen and unseen both so clear,
Or simply that you stood beside me there?

As Easily As Trees

As easily as trees have dropped
Their leaves, so easily a man,
So unreluctantly, might drop
All rags, ambitions, and regrets
Today and lie with leaves in sun.
So he might sleep while they began,
Falling or blown, to cover him.

Distance and Peace

Go far enough away from anything
In time or space (and space is only time)
And you have peace. The clashes of the stars
Do not disturb the starlit night of earth.
And earthly wars if they are old enough
Make restful reading to a man in bed.

And so with distance that is neither space
Nor time. The grass we walk upon is peaceful.
We can lie down on it and go to sleep,
Being too far above it ever to feel
The toil and competition of the roots,
Their struggle, slow frustration and defeat.

Statement

I follow Plato only with my mind.
Pure beauty strikes me as a little thin,
A little cold, however beautiful.

I am in love with what is mixed, impure,
Doubtful and dark and hard to disencumber.
I want a beauty I must dig for, search for.

Pure beauty is beginning and not end.
Begin with sun and drop from sun to cloud,
From cloud to tree, from tree to earth itself,

And deeper yet down to the earth-dark root.
I am in love with what resists my loving,
With what I have to labor to make live.

Fair and Unfair

The beautiful is fair, the just is fair.
Yet one is commonplace and one is rare,
One everywhere, one scarcely anywhere.

So fair unfair a world. Had we the wit
To use the surplus for the deficit,
We'd make a fairer fairer world of it.

Flower and Bee

With wisdom for our wonder
The flower and the bee
In a world designed for plunder
Have reciprocity.

For the bee takes from the flower
What the flower wants to give,
And the bee gives to the flower
What the flower takes to live.

Though the plan is less than loving,
Though the ethic is not soaring,
How far better than our living
When our loving turns to warring.

Unanimity

On shipboard and far out at sea
Two sat in deck chairs drawn together
Reading the same book silently
Day after day of even weather.

One held the book for both to read
And turned the page when it was read—
Two minds so equal and agreed
That nothing needed to be said.

The Good Life

The river plunges to the spillway floor
Then slides into a pool, and here the bathers
Plunge from the rocks and climb back on the rocks—
A hundred, more than a hundred sons of Adam
From smooth small boys a sculptor might have done
In a few strokes, to slowly hammered men
From buff to bronze. They have been here before.

Factories face both banks, but the river is wide
And factory windows might as well be blind.
No one comes down the river for the falls.
No one comes up the river for the rocks.
Here is a space the city cannot get,
Reserved for do-as-you-please and plenty-of-room
And plenty-of-time. In short, for the good life.

Seven daredevils are climbing up the falls
Like high-relief half in, half out of water.
They reach a certain point but not above;
The spillway curves too steep. They pause, they poise,
They cling to the rushing curtain, then climb down.
Off by himself a fat man sleeps in the sun,
Hands over belly, newspaper over face.
F
Five youths sit on a flat slab playing cards.
If one game ends and another game begins,
If someone loses and if someone wins,
Somebody else will have to say. A boy
Stands by the pool edge with a fishing pole.
I watch awhile, but if he gets a fish
Or gets a bite, somebody else must tell.

Nobody hurries, nobody hesitates.
Nobody interferes, nobody stares.
Nobody gives commands or calls Come home,
Or if they do nobody seems to hear.
Nobody misses her, nobody cares.
No clock in sight except the tolerant sun.
And there is sun enough and sun to spare.

Neighbors are those who share one piece of soap
Like those two lathering each other's back.
Before they plunge to rinse, they cross themselves.
Why do they cross themselves? Where is the evil
Here where the river pours upon the rocks
And sun pours on the rocks and on the river?
Here is no Eve. Here is no little snake.

On That Cool Plane

On that cool plane conflict is harmony
And what was discord now is dissonance,
Part of the music, the moving part of music.

And if the resolution is delayed
Bar after bar, or if one dissonance
Shifts to another and then shifts again,

We are not anxious for the resting chord.
It comes, it comes in time. Solved and unsolved
On that cool plane are equal in delight.

Preparation

Last fall I saw the farmer follow
The plow that dug the long dark furrows
Between the hillslope and the hollow.

All winter long the land lay fallow.
The woodchuck slept within his burrow
And heard no hound or farm boy's hallow.

Tonight the rain drives its dark arrows
Deep in the soil, down to its marrow.
The arrows of the sun tomorrow.

Two Glories

Before it set the searchlight sun
Broke through a narrow slit of heaven,
And what all day it hadn't done
It did in one brief quarter hour,
And all the light it hadn't given
It gave with all the purer power.
Two glories fell on us as one:
The rising sun, the setting sun.

His Own

The fish leaps up to take the fly,
The bird dives down to take the fish.
Seldom we see the plunder die
But sometimes hear the sudden splash

And turn in time to catch the flash
Before we see what we have seen.
And who is he who would not wish
His own to be as quick and clean?

True North

The needle has its north but not true north
For its direction
Wanders and constantly requires correction.

Nor is the star whose name is north true north
Though it turns near
The pole of the celestial hemisphere.

Nothing that we can follow is true north,
Nothing we see,
Being a point in pure geometry.

159

And even—so I understand—true north
Does not stay true
But slowly travels in a circle too.

Perhaps it would be true to say true north
Does not exist
Except to the extreme idealist.

But for all ordinary needs of north
Compass and star
Are north enough to guide the mariner.

What Has to Be

How flawlessly
What has to be
Becomes and is.

All that he was before
A man is more and more.

And if he imitate,
That too is fate,
That too is his.

Though he rebel and break away
His disobedience must obey.

Rocking Boulder

Despite its age, despite its weight
This boulder serves to demonstrate
The instability of hate.

What held it rigid wore away
Until an age, until a day
When children rocked it in their play.

Past and Future

They do not see what I have done,
Only what I have yet to do.
The way they say If I were you
Implies I hardly have begun.

The future often is so clear
To anyone with eyes to see,
However dim the past may be
To anyone who wasn't here.

Seagulls

Between the under and the upper blue
All day the seagulls climb and swerve and soar,
Arc intersecting arc, curve over curve.

And you may watch them weaving a long time
And never see their pattern twice the same
And never see their pattern once imperfect.

Take any moment they are in the air.
If you could change them, if you had the power,
How would you place them other than they are?

What we have labored all our lives to have
And failed, these birds effortlessly achieve:
Freedom that flows in form and still is free.

1950

The Face against the Glass

Part for the Whole

When others run to windows or out of doors
To catch the sunset whole, he is content
With any segment anywhere he sits.

From segment, fragment, he can reconstruct
The whole, prefers to reconstruct the whole,
As if to say, I see more seeing less.

A window to the east will serve as well
As window to the west, for eastern sky
Echoes the western sky. And even less—

A patch of light that picture-glass happens
To catch from window-glass, fragment of fragment,
Flawed, distorted, dulled, nevertheless

Gives something unglassed nature cannot give:
The old obliquity of art, and proves
Part may be more than whole, least may be best.

The Dandelion Gatherer

Bulging in petticoats in May she comes
Barefoot or in old bursting shoes, her hair
Bandanna'd and her ears hooped down with gold,
Bearing a gunnysack with no one knows
How many thousand martyred golden heads
—Phoebus Apollo, Dionysus, Christ—
All lost, all plundered, severed, and all saved:
The gleaming wineglass and the golden wine.

Squash in Blossom

How lush, how loose, the uninhibited squash is.
If ever hearts (and these immoderate leaves
Are vegetable hearts) were worn on sleeves,
The squash's are. In green the squash vine gushes.

The flowers are cornucopias of summer,
Briefly exuberant and cheaply golden.
And if they make a show of being hidden,
Are open promiscuously to every comer.

Let the squash be what it was doomed to be
By the old Gardener with the shrewd green thumb.
Let it expand and sprawl, defenceless, dumb.
But let me be the fiber-disciplined tree

Whose leaf (with something to say in wind) is small,
Reduced to the ingenuity of a green splinter
Sharp to defy or fraternize with winter,
Or if not that, prepared in fall to fall.

Encounter

Those who have touched it or been touched by it
Or brushed by something that the vine has brushed,
Or burning it, have stood where the sly smoke
Has touched them—know the meaning of its name.

The leaf is smooth. Its green is innocence.
A clean, unblemished leaf, glossy when young.
A leaf the unobserving might overlook
And the observing find too prosperous.

I've seen a vine of it so old and crooked
It held a hen-coop in its grip, the stalk
Thick as a man's wrist. There it had grown,
Half out of sight, permitted, undisturbed.

Strangers to it, who on an autumn road
Have found a vine that swept a tree like fire
And gathered it barehanded and brought it home
For color, seldom gathered it again.

Some are immune and some have thought they were
And some, ever so cautiously with gloves,
Finding that it grew too near their homes,
Have tried to root it out and have succeeded

Except that something from the vine fastened
Upon their flesh and burned, and in a year
Or two the vine itself was there again,
Glossy and green and smooth and innocent.

My neighbor's cow grazing beside the road
Munches with joy (and almost with a smile)
The salad of its leaves, transmuting them
Into sweet milk that I will drink tomorrow.

Glass

Words of a poem should be glass
But glass so simple-subtle its shape
Is nothing but the shape of what it holds.

A glass spun for itself is empty,
Brittle, at best Venetian trinket.
Embossed glass hides the poem or its absence.

Words should be looked through, should be windows.
The best word were invisible.
The poem is the thing the poet thinks.

If the impossible were not,
And if the glass, only the glass,
Could be removed, the poem would remain.

Demonstration

With what economy, what indolent control
The hawk lies on the delicate air, looking below.
He does not climb—watch him—he does not need to climb.

The same invisible shaft that lifts the cumulus
Lifts him, lifts him to any altitude he wills.
Never his wings, only his scream, disturbs noon stillness.

Days of the sharp-cut cloud, mid-day, he demonstrates
Over and ever again the spiral. On smooth blue ice
Impeccable the figure-skater carves his curves.

Oh, how to separate (inseparable in the bird)
His altitude from his incessant livelihood:
His higher mathematics, his hunger on the ground.

Here by the Sea

Here by the prodigal and ever-pouring sea
The watcher has enough to watch, the sea being wide
Enough for the eye and wide and deep enough for the mind.
Between this coast and Spain is room for any ship
To be alone and long, whether in view or after,
And how far longer after. Surf for the shore-bound bather
Still renews, renews, and far as he would swim
The swimmer swims and back again. Here by the sea
The watcher walks or stands or lies bathed in clear space
While the white seabird forever skims the white-curled wave.

Fortune

Above the pool, above the place where water
Mirrors the green of grass, casually
The older man without apology
Leaned over and lifted his neighbor's foot.
And held it like a palmist in both hands.

"The lines say travel," he said. "So much is clear.
Little trips here and there—and one long journey."
He seemed to find a problem in the foot
Warm to the touch with sun's and its own warmth.
"The lines," he said, "say nothing of return.

They crisscross here like good and evil luck.
Crisscross and sometimes merge. But the foot's strength
I'd say was equal to any likely travel."
He gave the foot back to the casual
Grass above the dark reflective water.

The Spy

To leave his empty house yet not to leave it
But make himself a shadow at a window—
Who is this prowler private in the moonlight?

Then at another window and another,
His face against the glass and peering in—
What does he think he sees or wants to see?

Soft as the milkweed floss the September night.
White as the milkweed the untroubled moon
Whose face, though far, is also at the window.

Two faces, but the prowler peers in deeper
Spying upon the empty chair, spying
Upon the man who is and is not there.

The Amanita

Death never was concealed more coolly
(Hemlocks half-concealing the concealer)
But death is not the only apparition.

Between two darknesses, the rotting humus
Beneath, the boughs above, this not-candle
Unburning burns, the flesh white, cream, and crocus.

Are the flecks blemishes or some device
Of esoteric ironic beauty over
The finger-slender neck and fungal face

That all but blushes as if the thing concealed
Were not a poison coolly but a few drops
Or reminiscences of un-cool blood?

So recent out of earth, see how the earth
Still soils it with a few clean crumbs
Before the air has time to tarnish.

Bough-like, I bend above, but not to touch
(So easily the injurer is injured)
Its virginal gills, its veil, its breathing wax.

O World of Toms

O world of Toms—tomfools, Tom Peppers,
Dark Peeping Toms and Tom-the-Pipers,
Tom Paines, Tom Joneses, Tom Aquinases,
Undoubting Toms and Doubting Thomases,
Tomboys, Tom Thumbs, Tom-Dick-and Harries,
Tom Collinses and Tom-and-Jerries,
Tom Wolfes, Tom Jeffersons, Tom Hardies,
Tomcods, tomcats, tomtits, tom-turkeys—
O hospitable world! And still they come
In every shape and shade of Tom.

Portrait

Infinite learning, spiritual malaise
Of which as many phases as the moon's,
And universal critical acclaim
Conspire to bring him on the verge of age
To something verging on humility.
Having embraced the heresies one by one
He can afford now to affirm the faith
At no cost to his intellect or renown.
Having exhausted subtlety, he now
Would be plain-spoken, almost, on occasion.
Like a cold peak he rises out of mists
Which he once loved and, moonlit, still might love.
Or like an aging king secure enough,
Weary enough and proud enough to slight
His robes and humor some old dressing-gown.

Museum Birds

These birds that do not fly, though poised to fly,
Or having flown, have just this moment lighted,
The wings unfolded still, over the eggs
That, though they will not ever hatch, are safe
From hawks and snakes and owls, weasels and squirrels—

These birds, feathered as life, yet having escaped
At once life's fever and death's dissolution,
Untouched by frost, sleet, snow, rain, wind, heat, hail,
Warrings of many kinds, old age, disease,
The threat of hunger, the perils of migration—

These birds, balancing lightly on green twigs
That never will be anything but green,
Guarded by glass from dust, Time's fingerprint—
Ah happy twigs, ah happy, happy birds.

Superior Vantage

From the superior vantage of the bridge
We look down on the sunners, bathers, swimmers,
And on the innocently-azure water.

From the superior vantage of our knowledge
(Knowing the pollution of the river)
We ask, crossing the bridge, the ironic question:

How clean can one be washed in tainted water?
What is a sinner's profit, loss, and balance?
We ask, and lift our eyebrows for an answer.

Above the arching bridge our arching brows.
Ah, but the ignorant, unfastidious bathers
Still dip and dive and swim and float unbothered.

The Big Tent

Amid fanfares aloft the Incredible Unus
Upside-down and poised on one forefinger
Upon a globe upon a pedestal
Radiates to the circumambient crowd
Apt and vicarious equanimity,
While apropos in another part of the tent
A man eats fire without getting burnt
And the caged monkeys begin to be amused.

Meanwhile the eagle poises for his act,
In one claw thirteen arrows clasped
And in the other an iron olive branch
With thirteen leaves and thirteen iron olives,
While all the regimented doves
Wheel up and flash in aerial dress parades
And one old irrepressible parrot screams:
"A plot! A plot! Hell's bells! E pluribus unum!"

Just then, amid concussive brasses,
The presidential party take their seats.

The Heiress

The orchestra among the palms, a boy
Bearing like a cold Torch of Liberty
A bottle on a tray above his head—
Just then the matched-pearl necklace broke. "Police!"
She screamed. "Don't anybody dare to move."
Crouching upon the floor like a frantic hen,
She tried to scoop them, all the scattered pebbles,
Into her crazy Nineteen Hundred skirt.
The music stopped. The boy froze like a dancer.
Perfectly timed the manager and three
Detectives darted in (Please everybody
Keep your seats) and fell on hands and knees.
They counted, "Fifty, fifty, fifty-one."
"But there were fifty-two," she moaned. "Oh God!"
Somebody kicked at something with his toe
And it rolled out in view. Now God be thanked,
Old woman, your pearls and you are saved and safe.
Praise God from whom all blessings flow. Praise Him
All creatures here below. The boy, bending,
Sets Liberty upon the table cloth.
Again the orchestra among the palms.

The Buzz Plane

May my Irish grandfather from Tyrells Pass
Grant me the grace to make a proper curse on you, accursed!
You who on a holy Sabbath or a fair holiday
Buzz and circle above my head like the progeny
Of the miscegenation of a buzzard and a bumble-bee.

The great bombers I hate with a lofty hatred,
But you, Harpy, with your unspeakable clatter,
Your sputtering, stuttering, and you know what,
Queering both my music and my silence,
I despise as the perfection of pure nuisance.

Where is the wind-wailed island of mist and seagulls,
Where is the mountain crag mounting to eagles,
Where is the saint's cell, the hermit's citadel,
The nine bean rows and the hive for the honey bee,
Safe from your snoopings, swoopings, and defilements?

May your wife be a gad, a goad, and a gadfly.
May all your bawling, brawling brats never leave you peace.
May you grow bald and birds defile your head.
May your flights be tailspins and your landings crashes.
Fie, fie, fie on you! And the word has power!

The Hawk

Who is the hawk whose squeal
Is like the shivering sound
Of a too tightly wound
Child's toy that slips a reel?

But beyond who is why.
Why any cry at all
Since death knows how to fall
Soundlessly from the sky?

Babylon and Babel

For what was dark and vast
Man used to read the past.

Two words he brooded on
Were Babel and Babylon—

The tower that rose so steep,
The town that sank so deep.

But words and worlds decay.
Where are those two today?

Tame as an infant's fable
Are Babylon and Babel.

Not with the dusty dead
But now and overhead
Our darkness and our dread.

Patior

"I suffer," says the Latin.
"I wait and suffer," says the patient man.
"I suffer and refuse to wait," the passionate man.

"My suffering will not let me wait," says passion.
"My waiting is my suffering," says the man of patience.
The Latin does not say who suffers more.

But I can say who suffers most: he
For whom the waiting and the not waiting
Are the twin talons of a bird of prey.

Peace

Blue porcelain, bronze Buddha, Buddha of stone
Beaming and benignant as the moon—
Light in the gallery is late afternoon
And momentarily I am alone.

Peace within peace, the peace of Buddha's smile,
The peace of sculptors in some sheltered place
Smoothing the last flaw from the smiling face,
And here for me, peace for a little while.

Yet even while the craftsman curved these lips,
At that same moment of impervious peace,
Other men, somewhere, crumpled to their knees,
Broken and bloody underneath the whips.

175

Hide-and-Seek

Here where the dead lie hidden
Too well ever to speak,
Three children unforbidden
Are playing hide-and-seek.

What if for such a hiding
These stones were not designed?
The dead are far from chiding;
The living need not mind.

Too soon the stones that hid them
Anonymously in play
Will learn their names and bid them
Come back to hide to stay.

Dog-Day Night

Just before night darkens to total night
A child at the next farm is calling, calling,
Calling her dog. Heat and the death of wind
Bring the small wailing like a mosquito close.
Will nothing stop her? Yet my complaining adds
To my complaint. Welcome it like a bird,
A whippoorwill, I say, closing my windows
North and east. The voice evades the glass.
She will not, will not let the dog be lost.
Why don't they tell her, isn't she old enough
To hear how the whole dog-gone earth is loose
And snooping through the dark and won't come home?

The Strewing Herbs

Here are the herbs against disease and death
The warped hands of old women used to strew
At candled wakes or in plague-haunted rooms,
The herbs of lazar-houses, gaols, and tombs,
Wormwood and tansy, santolina, rue.

Expect no sweetness here. Rather a scent
Bitter-to-burning, clean, permanent.
By stonestep, wall or well gravely they grow,
Prophylactic against the day of doom
For the few poking wayfarers who know.

The Faultless Dead

How faultlessly well bred
Are the exemplary dead
Who never ask for more,
Who never slam a door,
Who make no needless noise
Or ever lose their poise.
Gossip they seldom hear.
For slander, a deaf ear.
Never the questioner,
How they defer, defer.

Remind Me of Apples

When the cicada celebrates the heat,
Intoning that tomorrow and today
Are only yesterday with the same dust
To dust on plantain and on roadside yarrow—
Remind me, someone, of the apples coming,
Cold in the dew of deep October grass,
A prophecy of snow in their white flesh.

In the long haze of dog days, or by night
When thunder growls and prowls but will not go
Or come, I lose the memory of apples.
Name me the names, the goldens, russets, sweets,
Pippin and blue pearmain and seek-no-further
And the lost apples on forgotten farms
And the wild pasture apples of no name.

Two Words

Two words are with me noon and night
Like echoes of the solitude
That is my home—half field, half wood,
Feldeinsamkeit, Waldeinsamkeit.

In words as quiet as the Psalms
I hear, I overhear the tone
Of Concord and of Emerson,
And all the autumn mood of Brahms.

However foreign to my tongue
They are familiar to my mind
As is the breathing of the wind
And all the wind has said and sung.

The Alchemist

Old scientific saint of sorts,
Arab or Alexandrian,
As devious as diligent,
Testing your Plato in retorts
And out of base devising bright—
Give me a clew, a word, a hint,
A nod, you old Egyptian boy.

As if you could, poor credulous quack
Whose toil was child's play since for you
Color of gold was good as gold.
I want the actual element:
Atomic number, atomic weight.
From the alembic of my lack
Not gilt, by God, but gold, gold joy.

Weathervane

Moving unmoved,
Like the fixed tree
For constancy
But like the leaf
Aware
Of all the tricks
And politics
Of air.

Fickle?
Let the fool laugh
Who fails to see
That only he
Who freely turns
Discerns,
Moving unmoved
Is free.

Gloria

Bach praising God the Father we now praise
Who praise no more the Father. We now praise
Our Father Bach, Our praise is for his praise
Of God the Father. Ah, but praising him
Do we not praise with him our Father God?
For praise itself is God and praise the Father.

Thistle Seed in the Wind

Pioneer, paratrooper, missionary of the gospel seed,
Discoverer, skylarker, parable of solitude,
Where is the mathematics, wisp, to tell your chance?
If when you fall you fail,
Are lost at last and die,
At least you will have made the great voyage out,
Your sun-saluting sail alone on the blue ocean-sky.
Hail, voyager, hail!

1960

The Orb Weaver

Gold

Suddenly all the gold I ever wanted
Let loose and fell on me. A storm of gold
Starting with rain a quick sun catches falling
And in the rain (fall within fall) a whirl
Of yellow leaves, glitter of paper nuggets.

And there were puddles the sun was winking at
And fountains saucy with goldfish, fantails, sunfish,
And trout slipping in streams it would be insult
To call gold and, trailing their incandescent
Fingers, meteors and a swimming moon.

Flowers of course. Chrysanthemums and clouds
Of twisted cool witch-hazel and marigolds,
Late dandelions and all the goldenrods.
And bees all pollen and honey, wasps gold-banded
And hornets dangling their legs, cruising the sun.

The luminous birds, goldfinches and orioles,
Were gone or going, leaving some of their gold
Behind in near-gold, off-gold, ultra-golden
Beeches, birches, maples, apples. And under
The appletrees the lost, the long-lost names.

Pumpkins and squashes heaped in a cold-gold sunset—
Oh, I was crushed like Croesus, Midas-smothered
And I died in a maple-fall a boy was raking
Nightward to burst all bonfire-gold together—
And leave at last in a thin blue prayer of smoke.

Swimmer

I

Observe how he negotiates his way
With trust and the least violence, making
The stranger friend, the enemy ally.
The depth that could destroy gently supports him.
With water he defends himself from water.
Danger he leans on, rests in. The drowning sea
Is all he has between himself and drowning.

II

What lover ever lay more mutually
With his beloved, his always-reaching arms
Stroking in smooth and powerful caresses?
Some drown in love as in dark water, and some
By love are strongly held as the green sea
Now holds the swimmer. Indolently he turns
To float.—The swimmer floats, the lover sleeps.

Farm Boy after Summer

A seated statue of himself he seems.
A bronze slowness becomes him. Patently
The page he contemplates he doesn't see.

The lesson, the long lesson, has been summer.
His mind holds summer as his skin holds sun.
For once the homework, all of it, was done.

What were the crops, where were the fiery fields
Where for so many days so many hours
The sun assaulted him with glittering showers?

Expect a certain absence in his presence.
Expect all winter long a summer scholar,
For scarcely all its snows can cool that color.

Tomatoes

Nature and God by some elusive yet felicitous
Division of labor that I do not comprehend
(Salts of the soil, rain, the exuberant August sun,
Omniscience, omnipresence, and omnipotence)
Contrived these gaudy fruits, but I was the gardener
And in their lustihood, their hot vermilion luster,
Their unassailable three-dimensionality,
Their unashamed fatness, share the glory and fulfillment.

Now while the sacrificial knife is in abeyance
They bask and blaze serenely on the sun-splashed sill
For the last perfection of ripeness. A thank offering.
A peace offering. A still life. So still, so lifelike
The fruit becomes the painted picture of the fruit.

Floruit

Daringly, yet how unerringly
They bring to the cool and nun-like virtues
Of patience or something older than patience,
Silence, absolute silence, and obedience
All the hot virtues of the sun
And being wholly sex are wholly pure.

If with an equal candor we could face
Their unguarded faces, if we could look in silence
Long enough, could we touch finally,
We who when luckiest are said to flower,
Their fiery innocence, their day-long unabashed
Fulfillment, their unregretful falling?

185

High Diver

How deep is his duplicity who in a flash
Passes from resting bird to flying bird to fish,

Who momentarily is sculpture, then all motion,
Speed and splash, then climbs again to contemplation.

He is the archer who himself is bow and arrow.
He is the upper-under-world-commuting hero.

His downward going has the air of sacrifice
To some dark seaweed-bearded seagod face to face

Or goddess. Rippling and responsive lies the water
For him to contemplate, then powerfully to enter.

Boy Riding Forward Backward

Presto, pronto! Two boys, two horses.
But the boy on backward riding forward
Is the boy to watch.

He rides the forward horse and laughs
In the face of the forward boy on the backward
Horse, and *he* laughs

Back and the horses laugh. They gallop.
The trick is the cool barefaced pretense
There is no trick.

They might be flying, face to face,
On a fast train. They might be whitecaps
Hot-cool-headed,

One curling backward, one curving forward,
Racing a rivalry of waves.
They might, they might—

Across a blue of lake, through trees,
And half a mile away I caught them:
Two boys, two horses.

Through trees and through binoculars
Sweeping for birds. Oh, they were birds
All right, all right.

Swallows that weave and wave and sweep
And skim and swoop and skitter until
The last trees take them.

Exclusive Blue

Her flowers were exclusive blue.
No other color scheme would do.

Better than God she could reject
Being a gardener more select.

Blue, blue it was against the green
With nothing *not* blue sown or seen.

Yet secretly she half-confessed
With blue she was not wholly blessed.

All blues, she found, do not agree.
Blue riots in variety.

Purist-perfectionist at heart,
Her vision flew beyond her art—

Beyond her art, her touch, her power
To teach one blue to each blue flower.

Beyond Biology

Teased and titillated by the need
Always of something more than necessary,
Some by-product beyond biology,
The poet is like a boy poised on a rock
Who must produce an original waterfall,
Father a brook, or fertilize a tree.
Remember how young Gulliver quenched the fire?
Pure boy. Pure poet. The Lilliputian palace
Was saved, the emperor grateful, but the empress
(How like an empress) was implacably shocked.

Waxwings

Four Tao philosophers as cedar waxwings
chat on a February berrybush
in sun, and I am one.

Such merriment and such sobriety—
the small wild fruit on the tall stalk—
was this not always my true style?

Above an elegance of snow, beneath
a silk-blue sky a brotherhood of four
birds. Can you mistake us?

To sun, to feast, and to converse
and all together—for this I have abandoned
all my other lives.

Pitcher

His art is eccentricity, his aim
How not to hit the mark he seems to aim at,

His passion how to avoid the obvious,
His technique how to vary the avoidance.

The others throw to be comprehended. He
Throws to be a moment misunderstood.

Yet not too much. Not errant, arrant, wild,
But every seeming aberration willed.

Not to, yet still, still to communicate
Making the batter understand too late.

The Base Stealer

Poised between going on and back, pulled
Both ways taut like a tightrope-walker,
Fingertips pointing the opposites,
Now bouncing tiptoe like a dropped ball
Or a kid skipping rope, come on, come on,
Running a scattering of steps sidewise,
How he teeters, skitters, tingles, teases,
Taunts them, hovers like an ecstatic bird,
He's only flirting, crowd him, crowd him,
Delicate, delicate, delicate, delicate—now!

The Revelers

Hill after bumpkin hill blinking
wakes and wildweeds startle into flowers,
flowers into stars
unfrivolously winking
as fat ambassadorial bees
buzz in and out of embassies.

Tailored in moss-green satin
an old man indisputably of the old school,
silent in Latin,
perambulates the unruffled street
as if to demonstrate
paradigms of cool.

Then three young bucks, daisies above their ears,
bare-armed, bare-headed, breeze along
whistling as a glee to the god of weather
like a wind trio, in parts, a three-part song,
mobbed by envious and incredulous birds
in a musical dither.

Maples and elms bystanding laugh
a light leaf
to hear the wisecrack of a gun
from some inspired rapscallion.
Ceremonially a brick battalion
of chimneys salute the sun.

Hornpipes and hymns in mixed musicology,
Verdi from a green musicbox,
a fiddle hilarious with one string,
a deaconess with a sudden rage to sing
the doxology—
not to mention musical clocks.

A poem commissioned jointly by the Foundation for
Innocence in the Arts and the Fund for the Advance-
ment of Joy.

In pure voluptuousness people take off their shoes
to test the felicity of grass,
the luxury of lawns.
Dark girls turn dryad without trying
and boys of a certain cast impersonate fauns
and even try flying.

Infants with the gift of speech
talk to the larger flowers and, bending, listen.
One chick is filling a fluted squashblossom
for cornucopia with dewberries,
lowbush blueberries,
and all the red raspberries within reach.

And when the churchbells, firebells, cry noon,
picnics fit for an Eighteenth-Century picture,
buttermilk to overflowing,
dew-cold, butter-flecked and thick
enough to eat with a spoon,
and salads, salads that won't stop growing.

Wherever fountains, pools, puddles, or hoses
spill, urchins and nymphs undress
to their last pink roses
to put on glass or better than glass
beads of water
or something wetter.

And poets as guilelessly as running
boys catch butterflies in nets
catch butterflies and better than butterflies in verses
and, staking their virtuosity in punning,
open plump metaphorical purses
and make tall bets.

But one at an oriel, brooding and dreamy,
folds his poem-to-love in the form of a kite
or glider and, leaning, lets it go
down through the zigzag air, and so
(and so easily)
publishes it by giving it flight.

Elsewhere old Mrs. Goldthwaite wishing the unusual
touch to her herb tea,
flies to the hornet attic and comes down,
just as tinkling callers call,
in her (seacaptain's wife) grandmother's receiving gown
of cool pongee.

Mint, Mrs. Edlweiss, sage, or camomile?
Mint, please. Glory, how your teaspoons shine!
Purring Mrs. Goldthwaite pours. Meanwhile
old Mr. Goldthwaite puttering down cellar,
unmindful of any caller,
unearths a bottle of old elderflower wine.

The teadrinkers indoors hear the outdoor dancers
in shadows blue, shadows oblique,
dancers whose figurations open and close
like questions and answers.
Jack picks a daisy, dancing, with his toes
and little kids play hide-and-seek.

Till under the solemn moon they all turn silly
trying to catch the white milk in their hands
to spatter one another's faces,
running impossible races,
hunting the red tigerlily,
discovering undiscoverable lands.

But the moon, the moon stays sober and reaches
down, after a time, to touch them
coolly in white-curtained rooms—
the old like gothic carvings on old tombs,
the children not so much sleeping as enchanted
seashells on remote beaches.

The Seed Eaters

The seed eaters, the vegetarian birds,
Redpolls, grosbeaks, crossbills, finches, siskins,
Fly south to winter in our north, so making
A sort of Florida of our best blizzards.

Weed seeds and seeds of pine cones are their pillage,
Alder and birch catkins, such vegetable
Odds and ends as the winged keys of maple
As well as roadside sumac, red-plush-seeded.

Hi! with a bounce in snowflake flocks come juncos
As if a hand had flipped them and tree sparrows,
Now nip and tuck and playing tag, now squatting
All weather-proofed and feather-fluffed on snow.

Hard fare, full feast, I'll say, deep cold, high spirits.
Here's Christmas to Candlemas on a bunting's budget.
From this old seed eater with his beans, his soybeans,
Cracked corn, cracked wheat, peanuts and split peas, hail!

Dry Point

The undesigning yet designing snow
Lacking the art to rearrange, selects,
Selects nevertheless how artfully
Which of the little brittle winter bushes
And tall dry grasses it will delineate
And which conceal—the more selectively
The deeper the snow, the more effectively.
Oh, what a fine fastidious half-art.
Who would ask paint for it and not all dry point—
The burred accurate line—pure line, pure tone?

Confession

Whose every motion floats and flows
Undancing still the dancer dances
And dances in repose.

Heedless the poet drops a spark
On the most casual postal card
That burns a telltale mark.

In vain the lover wears a mask,
In vain denies, confessing more
Than the inquisitive ask.

Two Wrestlers

Two bronzes, but they were passing bronze before
The sculptor

All glint, all gleaming, face to face and grace
To grace

Balanced almost beyond their balance, tingling
To spring—

Who ever saw so point-by-point, so perfect
A pair

That either one—or both— or neither one—
Could win?

If this is trickery, the trick is smooth
In truth

One wrestler challenging—oh how unsafe—
Himself.

The Disengaging Eagle

There is a rumor
    the eagle tires of being eagle
    and would change wing
    with a less kingly bird as king,
    say, the seagull.

    With swans and cranes and geese,
    so the rumor goes,
    finding his official pose
    faintly absurd,
    he would aspire to unofficial peace
    and be, if possible, pure bird.

There is a rumor
    the eagle nurses now a mood
    to abdicate
    forever and for good
    as flagpole-sitter for the State.

    Is it the fall of age
    merely, a geriatrical complaint,
    this drift to disengage,
    this cool unrage?
    or rather some dark philosophic taint?

There is a rumor
    (God save us) the old warrior
    who screamed against the sun
    and toured with Caesar and Napoleon
    cavils now at war

    and would allegedly retire,
    resign, retreat
    to a blue solitude,
    an inaccessible country seat
    to fan a native fire
    a purely personal feud.

The Rock Climbers

In this soft age, in my soft
middle age, the rock climbers

Who giving all to love
embrace cold cliffs

Or with spread-eagle arms
enact a crucifixion

Hanging between the falling
and the not-attaining

Observed or unobserved
by hawks and vultures—

How vaulting a humility
superb a supererogation

Craggy to break the mind
on and to cool the mind.

Apple Peeler

Why the unbroken spiral, Virtuoso,
Like a trick sonnet in one long, versatile sentence?

Is it a pastime merely, this perfection,
For an old man, sharp knife, long night, long winter?

Or do your careful fingers move at the stir
Of unadmitted immemorial magic?

Solitaire. The ticking clock. The apple
Turning, turning as the round earth turns.

The Orb Weaver

Here is the spinner, the orb weaver,
Devised of jet, embossed with sulphur,
Hanging among the fruits of summer,

Hour after hour serenely sullen,
Ripening as September ripens,
Plumping like a grape or melon.

And in its winding-sheet the grasshopper.

The art, the craftsmanship, the cunning,
The patience, the self-control, the waiting,
The sudden dart and the needled poison.

I have no quarrel with the spider
But with the mind or mood that made her
To thrive in nature and in man's nature.

Two Bums Walk out of Eden

Two bums walk out of Eden. Evening approaches
The suave, the decorous trees, the careful grass,
The strict green benches—and the two bums go.

They caught the official nod, the backward-pointing
Thumb, and now they rise and leave a little
Briskly as men heedful to waste no time—

As men bending their steps toward due appointments.
The tall one looms like a skeleton; the runt
Walks with the totter of a tumbleweed.

Down the trimmed ceremonial path they go
Together, silent and separate and eyes
Ahead like soldiers. Down the long path and out.

What desert blanched these faces? What blowing sands
Gullied the eyes and scarred the hanging hands
While Babylon and Nineveh were falling?

Now a shade darker will be a shade less dark.
Now there is room for evening in the park
Where cool episcopal bells will soon be calling.

With the Year's Cooling

With the year's cooling come the colors of fire.
The later-blooming are the warmer flowers
That blaze and smolder in the thinning hours.

Now in the falling of the unfailing year
The quiet-clicking leaves unlatch a door
To those long landscapes we have waited for.

Bitter and fragrant hangs the smoke-tinged air
From some abandoned bonfire near or far,
While sterner night burns an intenser star.

Blue Jay

So bandit-eyed, so undovelike a bird
to be my pastoral father's favorite—
skulker and blusterer
whose every arrival is a raid.

Love made the bird no gentler
nor him who loved less gentle.
Still, still the wild blue feather
brings my mild father.

Ritual

Night comes no wilier inch-wise step-wise
shadow by shadow, tree by tree
than at the edge of night, single
and with exquisite circumspection
the ruffed grouse.

She has evaded, O how she
evades, the wildfire fox, the hound,
the sun's betrayal and the moon's
cold machinations.

Masked and peripheral she waits,
tingling with intimation, for one
more overtone of darkness against
her ritual supper on the snow—
the small gold maize.

Cypresses

At noon they talk of evening and at evening
Of night, but what they say at night
Is a dark secret.

Somebody long ago called them the Trees
Of Death and they have never forgotten.
The name enchants them.

Always an attitude of solitude
To point the paradox of standing
Alone together.

How many years they have been teaching birds
In little schools, by little skills,
How to be shadows.

Past Tense

Cool, rain-gray, classic, thin, the carved slate
Leans a little with age in two directions
But burdens not the dead with needless weight.

There was a time when death was satisfied
With small memento, such as a man could raise
Himself, if he wanted to, before he died—

With delicate willow and (without misgiving)
A verse of his own choosing, elegantly
Misspelled, to offer solace to the living.

Eighteen Hundred. I prefer past tense
In death—these few dark stones within a one-
Time white, long-unrepainted picket fence,

And three or four tall wind-torn wind-defying
Pines, and through the pines one smoke-blue hill
To give perspective to the fact of dying.

Desiring to Give All

Desiring to give all, to be all gift,
A living giver, then a giver dead,
He gave to friends the liveliness of his head,
Then stretching generosity with thrift,
Pondered if head itself, the clean bare skull,
Might not be saved and deeded to a friend
So that memorial and functional
Might thrive and blend
In an undying fate
As doorstop or as paper-weight.

Burial

Aloft, lightly on fingertips
As crewmen carry a racing shell—
But I was lighter than any shell or ship.

An easy trophy, they picked me up and bore me,
Four of them, an even four.
I knew the pulse and impulse of those hands,

And heard the talking, laughing. I heard
As from an adjoining room, the door ajar,
Voices but not words.

If I am dead (I said)
If this is death,
How casual, how delicate its masque and myth.

One pall bearer, the tenor, spoke,
Another whistled softly, and I tried to smile.
Death? Music? Or a joke?

But still the hands were there.
I rode half on the hands and half in air.
Their strength was equal to my strangeness.

Whatever they do (I said) will be done right,
Whether in earth and dark or in deep light,
Whatever the hands do will be well.

Suddenly I tried to breathe and cry:
Before you put me down, before
I finally die,

Take from the filing folders of my brain
All that is finished or begun—
Then I remembered that this had been done.

So we went on, on
To our party-parting on the hill
Of the blue breath, gray boulder, and my burial.

Epitaph

Believer he and unbeliever both
For less than both would have been less than truth.
His creed was godliness and godlessness.
His credit had been cramped with any less.

Freedom he loved and order he embraced.
Fifty extremists called him Janus-faced.
Though cool centrality was his desire,
He drew the zealot fire and counter-fire.

Baffled by what he deeply understood,
He found life evil and he found life good.
Lover he was, unlonely, yet alone—
Esteemed, belittled, nicknamed, and unknown.

The Aloof Peak

Over the level years the peak persuades me
With its aloofness, its cool disinclination
To be too patently in view, on view.

I acquiesce in its long un-veilings.
Wrapt and rapt in cloak and contemplation
It loses itself, a standing Socrates

For days and days. Or under its boughing Bo
Of cloud, Buddha the time-oblivious.
Only the little sightseer is rebuffed,

Busy and buzzing with his binoculars,
By so much otherworldliness, by so
Uncoy a coyness, so otherwise a wisdom.

Incognitio and incommunicado
It broods, while all the subsidiary hills
Camp like disciples at the foot, the feet.

Three Darks Come Down Together

Three darks come down together,
Three darks close in around me:
Day dark, year dark, dark weather.

They whisper and conspire,
They search me and they sound me
Hugging my private fire.

Day done, year done, storm blowing,
Three darknesses impound me
With dark of white snow snowing.

Three darks gang up to end me,
To browbeat and dumbfound me.
Three future lights defend me.

Sailboat, Your Secret

Sailboat, your secret. With what dove-and-serpent
Craft you trick the old antagonist.
Trick and transpose, snaring him into sponsor.

The blusterer—his blows you twist to blessing.
Your tactics and your tact, O subtle one,
Your war, your peace—you who defer and win.

Not in obeisance, not in defiance you bow,
You bow to him, but in deep irony.
The gull's wing kisses the whitecap not more archly

Than yours. Timeless and motionless I watch
Your craftsmanship, your wiles, O skimmer-schemer,
Your losses to profit, your wayward onwardness.

Hallelujah: A Sestina

A wind's word, the Hebrew Hallelujah.
I wonder they never give it to a boy
(Hal for short) boy with wind-wild hair.
It means Praise God, as well it should since praise
Is what God's for. Why didn't they call my father
Hallelujah instead of Ebenezer?

Eben, of course, but christened Ebenezer,
Product of Nova Scotia (Hallelujah).
Daniel, a country doctor, was his father
And my father his tenth and final boy.
A baby and last, he had a baby's praise:
Red petticoat, red cheeks, and crow-black hair.

A boy has little say about his hair
And little about a name like Ebenezer
Except that he can shorten either. Praise
God for that, for that shout Hallelujah.
Shout Hallelujah for everything a boy
Can be that is not his father or grandfather.

But then, before you know it, he is a father
Too and passing on his brand of hair
To one more perfectly defenseless boy,
Dubbing him John or James or Ebenezer
But never, so far as I know, Hallelujah,
As if God didn't need quite that much praise.

But what I'm coming to—Could I ever praise
My father half enough for being a father
Who let me be myself? Sing Hallelujah.
Preacher he was with a prophet's head of hair
And what but a prophet's name was Ebenezer,
However little I guessed it as a boy?

Outlandish names of course are never a boy's
Choice. And it takes time to learn to praise.
Stone of Help is the meaning of Ebenezer.
Stone of Help—what fitter name for my father?
Always the Stone of Help however his hair
Might graduate from black to Hallelujah.

204

Such is the old drama of boy and father.
Praise from a grayhead now with thinning hair.
Sing Ebenezer, Robert, sing Hallelujah!

Catch

Two boys uncoached are tossing a poem together,
Overhand, underhand, backhand, sleight of hand, every hand,
Teasing with attitudes, latitudes, interludes, altitudes,
High, make him fly off the ground for it, low, make him stoop,
Make him scoop it up, make him as-almost-as-possible miss it,
Fast, let him sting from it, now, now fool him slowly,
Anything, everything tricky, risky, nonchalant,
Anything under the sun to outwit the prosy,
Over the tree and the long sweet cadence down,
Over his head, make him scramble to pick up the meaning,
And now, like a posy, a pretty one plump in his hands.

Come Out into the Sun

Come out into the sun and bathe your eyes
In undiluted light. On the old brass
Of winter-tarnished grass,
Under these few bronze leaves of oak
Suspended, and a blue ghost of chimney smoke
Sit and grow wise
And empty as a simpleton.

The meadow mouse twitching her nose in prayer
Sniffs at a sunbeam like celestial cheese.
Come out, come out into the sun
And bask your knees
And be an acolyte of the illumined air.
The weathercock who yesterday was cold
Today sings hallelujah hymns in gold.

Soon the small snake will slip her skin
And the gray moth in an old ritual
Unseal her silk cocoon.
Come shed, shed now, your winter-varnished shell
In the deep diathermy of high noon.
The sun, the sun, come out into the sun,
Into the sun, come out, come in.

Monadnock

If to the taunting peneplain the peak
Is standpat, relic, anachronism,
Fossil, the peak can stand the taunt.

There was a time the peak was not a peak
But granite and resistant core,
Something that refused to wear

Away when time and wind and rivers wore
The rest away. Here is the thing
The nervous rivers left behind.

Endurance is the word, not exaltation.
Two words: endurance, exaltation.
Out of endurance, exaltation.

1965

Come Out into the Sun

Eagle Plain

The American eagle is not aware he is
the American eagle. He is never tempted
to look modest.

When orators advertise the American eagle's
virtues, the American eagle is not listening.
This is his virtue.

He is somewhere else, he is mountains away
but even if he were near he would never
make an audience.

The American eagle never says he will serve
if drafted, will dutifully serve etc. He is
not at our service.

If we have honored him we have honored one
who unequivocally honors himself by
overlooking us.

He does not know the meaning of magnificent.
Perhaps we do not altogether either
who cannot touch him.

Able

Both to converse and to conserve
Frugal and fruitful, passionate-patient

Never mistaking facility for felicity
Salesmanship for craftsmanship

Skeptical of commendation or condemnation
This is the man.

Dolphin

In mythology the restraint shown by dolphins
Is praiseworthy. Foregoing the preposterous they are
Content with only a little more than
Truth. They do what actual-factual dolphins
Have been known to do in times
Past or times present: pilot a ship
Or ride a small boy bareback smiling.

Conversely real dolphins seem influenced by myth
As if the overheard story of Arion
Could furnish endless inspiration in a dolphin's
Daily life. Such was Opo of Opononi,
Opo of the Antipodes, Opo who let
Non-dolphin fellow bathers stroke his back.
And when he died New Zealand mourned.

Having achieved, after how many ages, dry
Land, these beasts returned to live successfully
With sharks and devilfish. Having achieved dry
Land they achieved the sea. And this
Was long long before the first myth.
Today the uninhabitable for us, thank Dolphin,
Is that much less uninhabitable and inhospitable.

In weather foggy-shaggy in mid-Atlantic
Watching their water sports, tumbling, leap-frog
Who could be wholly in the doldrums
Doleful? A rough sea chuckles with dolphins
And a smooth sea dimples. Delft blue.
Delphinium-blue blooming with white morning-glories.
The sea relaxes. They tickle the sea.

Love Conquered by a Dolphin could equally
Be called A Dolphin Conquered by Love.
The seabeast holds the god coiled
But his moony upward-rolling eyes tell
Who is the more hopelessly caught. Preposterous?
The antique sculptor shrugs: with so ravishing
A god what could poor dolphin do?

From the large brain intricate as man's
And slightly larger one could predict intelligence
And from intelligence superior to a dog's,
An ape's, an elephant's, one could predict
Language, but where is science to predict
(Much less explain) benevolence such as Opo's,
Opo riding a small boy bareback smiling?

Nothing less than forgiveness dolphins teach us
If we, miraculously, let ourselves be taught.
Enduring scientific torture no dolphin has yet
(With experimental electrodes hammered into its skull)
In righteous wrath turned on its tormentors.
What will science ever find more precious?
The sea relaxes. They bless the sea.

Coin Diver (Funchal)

He takes it first with his eye like a sparrow hawk
all the way down to water and a little way under.

Tossed out of heaven a dime is less than a dime
but silver larger than life in the diver's palm.

He holds it up. Larger than life and cleaner
than any money has a right to look.

He taps his forehead to salute the donor
who over the rail from under the clouds peers.

Another coin cuts water. Cat-wise he waits,
he waits for stillness and a certain depth

Then with the least fuss possible he follows
but loses it this time, poor deep blue devil.

But does he? Does he? His innocent palms are empty.
He grins: the silver safe between his toes.

Triple Guard

Those who are fond of knocking off marble
fingers and more than fingers here confront
unknockable bronze.

He can defend himself, this youth.
Beyond and within his superhuman hardness
his fists are ready.

And something more—being too calm
too perfect not to rebuff (while he allures)
the plundering eye.

Irreproachable, unapproachable,
self-contained and safe for a long time yet,
a long time yet.

Sniper

The tree becomes him, he becomes the tree—
A visionary whom the world can't see.

His solitude makes sense.
His leisure is immense.

Least organized of men and most unknown,
His deaths are singular, including his own.

How lean, how lyrical
A life. A fame how small.

Hogwash

The tongue that mothered such a metaphor
Only the purest purist could despair of.

Nobody ever called swill sweet but isn't
Hogwash a daisy in a field of daisies?

What beside sports and flowers could you find
To praise better than the American language?

Bruised by American foreign policy
What shall I soothe me, what defend me with

But a handful of clean unmistakable words—
Daisies, daisies, in a field of daisies?

The Articles of War

Do I forget the Articles of War?
Herded into a bare mess hall
We stood against the unaccommodating wall
Or squatted on the floor
To hear what they could hang or shoot us for.

All of us green, but one greener by half,
Green enough to stand out in the crowd,
Asked (since questions were allowed)
"Can you resign from the Army?" The laugh
We gave him! How we hooted at the calf!

Hootable, I suppose, was Henry Thoreau
Whose equally unaccommodating fate
It was to try to disentangle from the State.
But Liberty would not let him go.
The State said: "Henry, no."

Somebody next, who knows? may try
Resigning from the human race,
Somebody aghast at history,
Haunted by hawk's eyes in the human face.
Somebody—could it be I?

The Black Hood

You don't remember—or perhaps you do—
The man who hid his head in the black hood
And worked a miracle or thought he could
To prove them one: the beautiful and the true?
He made you look, for once, the way you should:
Highly presentable yet no less you.

How we elude the harsh antinomies.
In love with two worlds that can scarcely meet
How human to claim both, the best of both,
To ask for dream fulfillment *and* for truth,
A likeness, but a flattering likeness, please.
Oh, never call the heart's desire deceit.

We could be less, a shade the less, to blame
Because our betters nobly do the same:
Bland Plato pulling on his long black hood
To find identical the true, the good,
Proving the world is better than we know
Because we and great Plato wish it so.

How much hood-hiding not to say hood-winking,
Yet with what lofty motives we deceive.
How many times we think that we are thinking
In making believe we do not make believe.
We spend to save—or do we save to spend?
We are the Russians' enemy and friend.

If I were gold, I would endow a chair
On principle if not for practical good
For someone who could tell us how to tell
Clean truth from trick, someone who dared to tell,
Someone as uncommitted as fresh air,
Without a trace, without a thread, of hood.

Good God, what have I said? And who am I?
You might suppose me totally unacquainted
With the dark mysteries of Paradox.
I am a poet, minor. Or I try.
If all duplicity deserves a pox,
Then I myself am tainted, more than tainted.

I marry freedom to fastidious form.
I trust the spirit in the arms of sense.
I can contrive a calm from any storm.
My art, my business is ambivalence.
In every poem by me on my shelf
Confidentially yours I hide myself.

Thus do I praise duplicity and damn it.
I hate equivocation and I am it.
True though I hanker for simplicity,
The concept of plain truth, plain simple truth,
Seems quaint and dubious as a wisdom tooth.
How guileless that black hood compared to me.

Written for and read at the literary exercises of the Harvard
Chapter of Phi Beta Kappa, June 13, 1960.

Metal and Mettle

The slow laborer and the speedy athlete
it would be hard to choose between
for the esthetic satisfaction of watching.

One bronze back is pushing
a wheelbarrow level with cement up
an inclined gangplank steadily

the center line of the back undulating
at each step like a cobra delicately
dancing to the flute.

Metal for hardness, for sheen, for
durability but for man the word is mettle
a variant of metal.

What does the athlete finally have?
At best a victory but the laborer
has a new building, a building built.

Watching Gymnasts

Competing not so much with one another
As with perfection
  They follow follow as voices in a fugue
  A severe music.

Something difficult they are making clear
Like the crack teacher
  Demonstrating their paradigms until
  The dumb see.

How flower-light they toss themselves, how light
They toss and fall
  And flower-light, precise, and arabesque
  Let their praise be.

Riddler

He comes out as a brook comes out of snow
From no identifiable address,
And you nor I nor anyone else can guess
Where he is going, where he is going to go.

His name is Huckleberry, alias John.
He'll sail you (if he had it) any craft
Such as a Mississippi-going raft
And when the big waves hit him, he'll hang on.

Gun-metal water with a gleam of sun
Matches his eye but not his devil-may-care.
He leaps from silence into shout to dare
What anyone else has done, or hasn't done.

Always a trace of riddle on his lips
Curled half in amity, half in defiance.
Jack-the-Giant-Killer (given the giants)—
He is the boy who stows away on ships.

Old Man's Confession of Faith

The blowing wind I let it blow,
I let it come, I let it go.

Always it has my full permission.
Such is my doctrinal position.

I let it blow, I more than let it,
I comfort give, aid and abet it.

Young long ago I would resist it.
Today, full circle, I assist it.

When the wind blows, I let it blow me.
Where the wind goes, why there I go me.

I teach the wind no indoor manners
But egg it on with flags and banners.

Whether it expedite or slow me
When the wind blows I let it blow me.

Blow long, blow late, blow wild, blow crazy
Blow paper bag, blow dust, blow daisy

Blow east, blow west—I let it blow.
I never never tell it No.

Skier

He swings down like the flourish of a pen
Signing a signature in white on white.

The silence of his skis reciprocates
The silence of the world around him.

Wind is his one competitor
In the cool winding and unwinding down.

On incandescent feet he falls
Unfalling, trailing white foam, white fire.

Condor

How flawless and unvarying his candor
Over the wide, over the high Andes
The great condor

So infinitely far from all dissembling.
Is there a doubt? He dares, he dares the sun
To watch him

And the sun watches. Watches, watches the condor
Over the wide, over the high Andes
With equal candor.

Astronomer

Far far
Beyond the stargazer
The astronomer

Who does not try
To make the sky
His sky

But goes out of his mind
To find
Beyond.

Nightly he goes
Nightly he knows
Where no comfort is

And this
His comfort is
His irreducible peace.

Uncanny traveler
To leave himself how far
Behind.

Eagle Soaring

Only in the perfection of his calligraphy
With its classic loops and severe flourishes,
The scribe inseparable from his inscription,
The writer and the writing one, moving
As slowly as a slowed moving picture—

Only in the strict dance, the passacaglia
Endlessly repeating endless variations,
Grave as a ceremonial saraband
For which the clouds are choreographers,
The wings taut with formality and formal ease—

Above all in the complete undistraction
And extreme loneliness of his observational
From which he bows and broods on the round world,
Turning as if in imitation of her turning,
Obedient to nothing but the pure act of seeing—

Enviable

Enviable, not envious, the little worm
Whose apple is his world and equally his home,
Who at his feasting hears no hint of doom.

Deep, deep in love he is, who could be deeper in?
He envies no one, he could envy whom?
I envy no one, I could envy him.

Emergence

If you have watched a moulting mantis
With exquisite precision and no less
Exquisite patience, extricate itself
Leaf-green and like a green leaf clinging
Little by little, leg by leg
Out of its chitin shell, you likewise know
How one day coaxes itself out of another
Slowly, slowly by imperceptible degrees
Of gray, and having fully emerged, pauses
To dry its wings.

Delicate the Toad

Delicate the toad
Sits and sips
The evening air.

He is satisfied
With dust, with
Color of dust.

A hopping shadow
Now, and now
A shadow still.

Laugh, you birds
At one so
Far from flying

But have you
Caught, among small
Stars, his flute?

Museum Vase

It contains nothing.
We ask it
To contain nothing.

Having transcended use
It is endlessly
Content to be.

Still it broods
On old burdens—
Wheat, oil, wine.

Aphrodite as History

Though the marble is ancient
It is only an ancient
Copy and though the lost
Original was still more ancient
Still it was not Praxiteles
Only a follower of Praxiteles
And Praxiteles was not first.

Stellaria

Your five white, frost-white
Petals and plum-purple stamens
Stellaria, for a sharp eye
For a fond eye— who
But the botanist ever sees?

Your foliage is weed familiar
But your flower is almost
Like a fairy princess invisible.
Better so. Those who escape
Man's notice escape man's scorn.

221

To the most proper garden
You come uninvited and unthanked
Before or after the planted
Plants, schooled for an early
Winter and a late spring.

Easier larger flowers than you
I would not slander. Under
The sun all are equal.
And yet your very smallness
Like modesty is a jewel.

For I am not unprejudiced.
The unpromoted flower I prefer
Far from a florist window
As you, starwort, are far.
How cool, unqualified, your gaze.

The Forced Forsythia

Even the florist if he dreams of force
(Dreaming of sudden fortune) is only dreaming.
His warmth, his moisture, must be love, of course.

Women, true, have been goaded by the gods
In guise of bull or swan. Still they lack power,
The very gods, to force a flower to flower.

A yellow any more yellow would dazzle eyes.
Loaded, bursting with it, the wands are bowing
While snow peers through the glass in cold surprise.

Idyl of Lake Reedy

Others have moved the heavens
To move but what other
With more idyllic ease (herself
Unmoving) than Miss Lillie Stoate
Who merely sat by water?

Any considerable body of water
Would serve if Miss Lillie
Happily were sitting beside it.
Simply sitting there. What was
It Brancusi said about simplicity?

Miss Lillie Stoate from Mississippi
Came to fruit-growing Florida
And sat beside Lake Reedy
Several hours several successive days.
Noted, she brought her umbrella.

A big black one undoubtedly.
In this foreseeable unforeseeable world
Any woman of sixty-seven
Knows she needs ample protection.
She also brought her knitting

Most probably though not noted.
Difficult indeed to picture her
Without it—sitting and knitting
Knitting and sitting. Oh, sometimes
She simply sat and watched

The stilt-legged water-birds
Dip and dive and dimple
A surface otherwise all unruffled
And uneventful. Was Lake Reedy
Named for somebody named Reedy?

However so, at this distance
We are privileged to picture
Lake Reedy a really reedy
Lake fringed with water-weeds
And bulrushes and various grasses.

223

Prayer must have proved unavailing,
Prayer as if to waken
The Deity from afternoon napping.
Miss Lillie did not need,
Did not presume, to pray.

And what of cloud-compelling
Science? Had *that* been tried?
If so, we can legitimately
Label Miss Lillie Stoate both
Pre-scientific and post-scientific.

When the very first raindrops
A little hesitantly perhaps began
To fall on Lake Reedy
And on Miss Lillie, began
To stipple the bland surface

And the slightest possible stir
Of air to ripple it
She put down her knitting
And put up her umbrella
But kept on sitting. Why

Should she depart? Why should
She hurry away? The patter
Of drops on her umbrella
Was pleasant to listen to
Becoming more and more musical.

Only when it was clear
Beyond cavil that the rain
Meant business did Miss Lillie
Rise sighing, ah, surely less
From exertion than from fulfillment.

Ireland

which the sea refuses
to recognize as bona fide
land, the sea and all her watery clouds

and all her mewing gulls
"white craws as white as snaw"
that sweep, that sweep, that sweep

warm winter into cool summer
"rather cloudy, but with bright
periods in many places this morning"—

Ireland whose weather imitates
bird flightiness, imitates life,
imitates above all the Irish.

Comedian Body

Forgive comedian body
For featuring the bawdy.

For instance the poor fanny
So basic and so funny.

Forgive the penis pun
That perfect two-in-one.

Forgive the blowing nose.
Forgive the ten clown toes

And all the Noah's zoo
Of two by two by two.

Forgive a joke wherein
All love and art begin.

Forgive the incarnate word
Divine, obscene, absurd.

225

In Memoriam: Four Poets

I

Searock his tower above the sea,
Searock he built, not ivory.
Searock as well his haunted art
Who gave to plunging hawks his heart.

II

He loved to stand upon his head
To demonstrate he was not dead.
Ah, if his poems misbehave
'Tis only to defy the grave.

III

This exquisite patrician bird
Grooming a neatly folded wing
Guarded for years the Sacred Word.
A while he sang then ceased to sing.

IV

His head carved out of granite O,
His hair a wayward drift of snow,
He worshipped the great God of Flow
By holding on and letting go.

Thoreau in Italy

Lingo of birds was easier than the lingo of peasants—
they were elusive, though, the birds, for excellent reasons.
He thought of Virgil, Virgil who wasn't there to chat with.

History he never forgave for letting Latin
lapse into Italian, a renegade jabbering
musical enough but not enough to call music.

So he conversed with stones, imperial and papal.
Even the preposterous popes he could condone
a moment for the clean arrogance of their inscriptions.

He asked the Italians only to leave him in the past
alone, but this was what they emphatically never did.
Being the present, they never ceased to celebrate it.

Something was always brushing him on the street, satyr
or saint—impossible to say which the more foreign.
At home he was called touchy; here he knew he was.

Impossible to say. The dazzling nude with sex
lovingly displayed like carven fruit, the black
robe sweeping a holy and unholy dust.

Always the flesh whether to lacerate or kiss—
conspiracy of fauns and clerics smiling back
and forth at each other acquiescently through leaves.

Caught between wan monastic mountains wearing the tonsure
and the all-siren, ever-dimpling sea, he saw
(how could he fail?) at heart geography to blame.

So home to Concord where (as he might have known he would)
he found the Italy he wanted to remember.
Why had he sailed if not for the savour of returning?

An Italy distilled of all extreme, conflict,
collusion—an Italy without the Italians—
in whose green context he could con again his Virgil.

In cedar he read cypress, in the wild apple, olive.
His hills would stand up favorably to the hills of Rome.
His arrowheads could hold their own with art Etruscan.

And Walden clearly was his Mediterranean
whose infinite colors were his picture gallery.
How far his little boat transported him—how far.

Edith Sitwell Assumes the Role of Luna
or
If You Know What I Mean Said the Moon

Who (said the Moon)
Do you think I am and precisely who
Pipsqueak, are you

With your uncivil liberties
To do as you damn please?
Boo!

I am the serene
Moon (said the Moon).
Don't touch me again.

To your poking telescopes,
Your peeking eyes
I have long been wise.

Science? another word
For monkeyshine.
You heard me.

Get down, little man, go home,
Back where you come from,
Bah!

Or my gold will be turning green
On me (said the Moon)
If you know what I mean.

"Paper Men to Air Hopes and Fears"

The first speaker said
Fear fire. Fear furnaces
Incinerators, the city dump
The faint scratch of match.

The second speaker said
Fear water. Fear drenching rain
Drizzle, oceans, puddles, a damp
Day and the flush toilet.

The third speaker said
Fear wind. And it needn't be
A hurricane. Drafts, open
Windows, electric fans.

The fourth speaker said
Fear knives. Fear any sharp
Thing, machine, shears
Scissors, lawnmowers.

The fifth speaker said
Hope. Hope for the best
A smooth folder in a steel file.

The Packing Case

When Van Loon packed the human race
Neatly inside a packing case,
Dimensions one-half cubic mile—

When Van Loon poised the packing case
Over the upper edge of space
And teased and teetered it a while—

No one outside, no one bereft,
Not even one old Noah left
To mosey to the Land of Nod—

Sing lullaby—when history dived
And only geography survived—
Who mercifully breathed Thank God?

Time and the Sergeant

To take us in, bully and bawl us
Out was his official
Pleasure.

And he was beautifully built for it,
That buffed brass hair, that
Tuba voice

And those magnificent legs on which
He rocked he rocked. He never
Bent a knee.

How is the anal-oriented humor now?
Fresh and exuberant
As ever?

Or has Old Bastard Time touched
Even you, Sergeant,
Even you?

Cinna

Fourth Citizen: *Tear him for his bad verses.*

You were mistaken, Cinna, from the start.
First, to be single among sound married men,
Second, to make light of it. You were wrong there
And wrong again
On that red evening to have risked a breath of air.

But what was most conspicuously bad,
Being a poet, to let the thing be known.
And to have a name another man could have and had.
That, and to walk alone.

When the mob tore you, you were doubly torn:
Once for yourself, once for your art.
You were mistaken, Cinna, to be born.

Old Men

Weigh too much or weigh
Too little,

Settle into woodchucks or take
A fancy

To be feather-weight birds.
Very seldom

However you catch one singing.
As merchandise

Old men go very cheap
Marked down

Marked down year after year
After year.

Eagle Caged

Uneagled in his coop
Listless, lackluster
His idle feathers droop
Like a feather duster.

Wing that assumed the sky
Forgets to stir.
Even the diamond eye
Is prisoner.

The wan inner sheath
Closes, uncloses.
He blinks vaguely at death
And dying, dozes.

Icicles

Only a fierce
Coupling begets them
Fire and freezing

Only from violent
Yet gentle parents
Their baroque beauty.

Under the sun
Their life passes
But wait awhile

Under the moon
They are finished
Works of art

Poems in print
Yet pity them
Only by wasting

Away they grow
And their death
Is pure violence.

Come

As you are (said Death)
Come green, come gray, come white
Bring nothing at all
Unless it's a perfectly easy
Petal or two of snow
Perhaps or a daisy
Come day, come night.

Nothing fancy now
No rose, no evening star
Come spring, come fall
Nothing but a blade of rain
Come gray, come green
As you are (said Death)
As you are.

Reading Gravestones

I

These granite authorities on death
contradict one another as only
authorities can.

II

Squirrels in the oaks seem never
to have heard of death—
authorities on acorns.

III

After the mourners leave, the flowers
they leave could teach them
how to weep.

IV

Strange how the stones as they
grow heavier and more Egyptian
grow more taciturn.

V

Snow buries them a second time
as if one Christian burial
were not enough.

233

Siege

Indian-wise
We have kept moving in
With slant leaf-eyes
At windows room by room.
Your window-light is a light gloom now.
Isn't this what you wanted?

You've let us come, have watched us come
Until with any wind at all
Our hands brush on the outer wall
And brush again.
Your house is shadow-haunted.

You've let us come—
Give us a few years more
We'll undertake to bar and bind your door
To keep you always and forever home.
Isn't this what you wanted?

My Teachers Are the Centripetal Ones

The dervish turning in one timeless spot;
The thinker focusing the lens of thought;

The scholar in his self-convicted cell;
The saint God-centered and centripetal;

The watcher whose long motionlessness matches
The insect stillness of the thing he watches;

The marksman whose curled finger waits to move;
The lover, absent, aiming on his love.

1974

Like Ghosts of Eagles

The Mountain

does not move the mountain is not moved
it rises yet in rising rests and there
are moments when its unimaginable weight
is weightless as a cloud it does not come
to me nor do I need to go to it I only
need that it should be should loom always
the mountain is and I am I and now a cloud
like a white butterfly above a flower.

Like Ghosts of Eagles

The Indians have mostly gone
but not before they named the rivers
the rivers flow on
and the names of the rivers flow with them
    Susquehanna   Shenandoah

The rivers are now polluted plundered
but not the names of the rivers
cool and inviolate as ever
pure as on the morning of creation
    Tennessee   Tombigbee

If the rivers themselves should ever perish
I think the names will somehow somewhere hover
like ghosts of eagles
those mighty whisperers
    Missouri   Mississippi.

A Health to Earth

and her magnificent digestion
like a great cow she chews her cud
nothing defeats her   nothing escapes

237

the owl ejects an indigestible
pellet   earth ejects nothing
she who can masticate a mountain

what is a little junk to her
a little scrap   like a great cow
she chews it over   she takes her time

all man's perdurable fabrications
his structural steel, his factories, forts
his moon machines   she will in time

like a great summer-pasture cow
digest   in time assimilate
it all to pure geology.

Chimàphila, 1972

How easily I could have missed you
Your quiet blooming those July days
Noisy with the Democratic Convention

And all the other noises. All flowers
Are silent but some more so than others
And none more silent than Chimàphila

Whose petals are not sun-white daisy-white
But the subdued glow of forests
Dim with their dimness, a nodding flower.

A hundred blossoms and more I counted
Gathered in Quaker meeting, a hundred
Where in former years perhaps a dozen.

For you a late spring and a rainy summer
Must rate as blessing. How otherwise
Should Nineteen Seventy-two have been so banner?

Chimàphila, the winter-loving (so the Greek)
But oh how summer-loving when the still air
Lingers and broods over your intense sweetness.

Clearly whatever my woodland soil offers
Is all you ask, you of all flowers.
So I can say that you return my love.

Long after your petals fall and your fragrance
Is only in my mind, after deep snow
I will call up again and again your name.

Overhearing Two on a Cold Sunday Morning

We left our husbands sleeping,
Sun in our eyes and the cold air
Calling us out, yet not too cold
For winter to be rehearsing spring
At ten o'clock in the morning.

Like harps the telephone poles hum
And the glass insulators dazzle.
We left them warm in bed dreaming
Of primavera, dreaming no doubt
Of fountains, fauns, and dolphins.

Chickadees dance on the wind. They
Are young, our husbands, especially
As they lie sleeping. Sometimes
We imagine we are older than they
Though actually we're a little younger.

We have come up into the upper light.
We have come out into the outer air.
We could almost for a moment forget
Our husbands. No, that is not true.
Never for a moment can we forget them.

Soon we will go back to them and shout
"This is a beautiful day!" Or if
They are still sleeping, whisper it
Into their ears or on their lips.
We do not often leave them sleeping.

Prayer to A.N.W.
(Presuming on his name)

O towering peak O venerable pate
O snowfall beard O berg O bard
Send us your storms your Sturm-und-Drang
Let all your rhymes be winter rime
And smite and bless us with your wrath
O king philosopher-king O Alfred
Teach us to love the overwhelming
Then lull us lull us to sleep at last
Like infants cradled in the blast.

Silent Poem

backroad leafmold stonewall chipmunk
underbrush grapevine woodchuck shadblow

woodsmoke cowbarn honeysuckle woodpile
sawhorse bucksaw outhouse wellsweep

backdoor flagstone bulkhead buttermilk
candlestick ragrug firedog brownbread

hilltop outcrop cowbell buttercup
whetstone thunderstorm pitchfork steeplebush

gristmill millstone cornmeal waterwheel
watercress buckwheat firefly jewelweed

gravestone groundpine windbreak bedrock
weathercock snowfall starlight cockcrow

Blue Cornucopia

Pick any blue   sky-blue   cerulean   azure
cornflower   periwinkle   blue-eyed grass
blue bowl   bluebell   pick lapis lazuli
blue pool   blue girl   blue Chinese vase
or pink-blue chicory 'alias ragged sailor
or sapphire   bluebottle fly   indigo bunting
blue dragonfly or devil's darning needle
blue-green   turquoise   peacock   blue spruce
blue verging on violet   the fringed gentian
gray-blue   blue bonfire smoke   autumnal
haze   blue hill   blueberry   distance
and darker blue   storm-blue   blue goose
ink   ocean   ultramarine   pick winter
blue snow-shadows   ice   the blue star Vega.

November

Ruin of summer, wrecker of gardens,
A stingy sun, interminable rain—
Indicted, hailed into court, what do you say?

Balm for tired eyes my umber and grey embers,
My interlude between two brilliancies.
Time now for fireplace to grant the fire.

But in the woods, look, jewel-green my moss
And on each branch the strung beads of small buds
Ready for winter and for beyond winter.

December

Dim afternoon December afternoon
Just before dark, their caps
A Christmas or un-Christmas red
The hunters.

Oh, I tell myself that death
In the woods is far far better
Than doom in the slaughterhouse.
Still, the hunters haunt me.

Does a deer die now or does a hunter
Dim afternoon December afternoon
By cold intent or accident but always
My death?

History

I

History to the historian
Is always his story.

He puts the pieces
Of the past together

To make his picture
To make his peace—

Pieces of past wars
Pieces of past peaces.

But don't ask him
To put the pieces

Of the past together
To make your picture

To make your peace.

II

The Holy See is not by any means
the whole sea and the whole sea
so far as one can see is far from holy.

The Holy See is old but how much older
the sea that is not holy, how vastly
older the sea itself, the whole sea.

The Holy See may last a long time longer
yet how much longer, how vastly longer
the whole sea, the sea itself, the unholy sea

Scrubbing earth's unecclesiastical shores
as if they never never would be clean
like a row of Irish washerwomen

Washing, washing, washing away
far into the unforeseeable future
long after the Holy See no more is seen.

III

Henry Thoreau Henry James and Henry Adams
would never have called history bunk
not Henry James not Henry Adams.

Nor would Henry Adams or Henry James
ever have tried to get the boys
out of the trenches by Christmas.

Only Henry Thoreau might have tried
to get the boys out of the bunk out
of the Christmas out of the trenches.

For Henry Thoreau was anti-bunk Henry James
pro-bunk and what shall we say of Henry Adams
except that all four Henrys are now history?

IV

The great Eliot has come the great Eliot
has gone and where precisely are we now?

He moved from the Mississippi to the Thames
and we moved with him a few miles or inches.

He taught us what to read what not to read
and when he changed his mind he let us know.

He coughed discreetly and we likewise coughed;
we waited and we heard him clear his throat.

How to be perfect prisoners of the past
this was the thing but now he too is past.

Shall we go sit beside the Mississippi
and watch the riffraft driftwood floating by?

On a Theme by Frost

Amherst never had a witch
Of Coös or of Grafton

But once upon a time
There were three old women.

One wore a small beard
And carried a big umbrella.

One stood in the middle
Of the road hailing cars.

One drove an old cart·
All over town collecting junk.

They were not weird sisters,
No relation to one another.

A duly accredited witch I
Never heard Amherst ever had

But as I say there
Were these three old women.

One was prone to appear
At the door (not mine!):

"I've got my nightgown on,
I can stay all night."

One went to a party
At the president's house once

Locked herself in the bathroom
And gave herself a bath.

One had taught Latin, having
Learned it at Mount Holyoke.

Of course Amherst may have
Had witches I never knew.

The Bulldozer

Bulls by day
And dozes by night.

Would that the bulldozer
Dozed all the time

Would that the bulldozer
Would rust in peace.

His watchword
Let not a witch live

His battle cry
Better dead than red.

Give me the bullfinch
Give me the bulbul

Give me if you must
The bull himself

But not the bulldozer
No, not the bulldozer.

Cats

Cats walk neatly
Whatever they pick
To walk upon

Clipped lawn, cool
Stone, waxed floor
Or delicate dust

On feather snow
With what disdain
Lifting a paw

On horizontal glass
No less or
Ice nicely debatable

Wall-to-wall
Carpet, plush divan
Or picket fence

In deep jungle
Grass where we
Can't see them

Where we can't
Often follow follow
Cats walk neatly.

Line 1 is quoted from Olaus Murie, *Field Guide to Animal Tracks*,
The Peterson Field Guide Series (Boston, 1954), p. 113

Trade

The little man with the long nose
and the camera around his neck
has corn in his pocket for the pigeons
    not that he loves them.

The little man with the long nose
will put a little corn in your hand
for the pigeons if you will let him
        not that he loves you.

The pigeons will come and cluster
about your hand flapping and fanning
and feeding till not a kernel is left
        not that they love you.

And the little man with the long nose
will take your picture and you will
put a little something in his hand
        not that you love him either.

The Peacock

The over-ornate can be a burden as peacock
proves the weight of whose preposterous plumes
is psychological see how his peacock back is bent
hysterical he stamps his foot one more pavane
and I will scream he screams spreading once more
for the ten thousandth time that fantastic fan.

Picasso and Matisse
(circa 1950)

At Vallauris and Vence, Picasso and Matisse,
A trifling eighteen miles apart,
Each with his chapel, one to God and one to Peace,
Artfully pursue their art.

What seems, not always is, what is, not always seems,
Not always what is so is such.
The Party and the Church at absolute extremes
Are nearly near enough to touch.

247

At Vallauris and Vence, Picasso and Matisse,
One old, one older than before,
Each with his chapel, one to God and one to Peace,
Peacefully pursue their war.

The Two Lords of Amherst

The two Lords, Jeffery and Jehovah, side by side
Proclaim that hospitality lives and Jesus died.

Jeffery in whitewashed brick, Jehovah in gray stone
Both testify man does not live by bread alone.

From sacred love to bed and board and love profane
One could dart back and forth and not get wet in rain.

How providentially inclusive the design:
Here are the cocktails, here the sacramental wine.

Here is the holy, here the not-so-holy host.
Here are the potted palms and here the Holy Ghost.

Tell, if you can and will, which is more richly blest:
The guest Jehovah entertains or Jeffery's guest.

The Righteous

After the saturation bombing divine
worship after the fragmentation shells
the organ prelude the robed choir after
defoliation Easter morning the white
gloves the white lilies after the napalm
Father Son and Holy Ghost Amen.

The Pope

The Pope in Rome
Under St. Peter's dome
Is the Pope at home.

Pomp is his daily fare
Poised in his papal chair
Quite debonair.

The great bell pealing,
The cardinals kneeling,
The soaring ceiling—

All that display
Does not dismay
The Pope a single day.

Light Casualties

Light things falling—I think of rain,
Sprinkle of rain, a little shower
And later the even lighter snow.

Falling and light—white petal-fall
Apple and pear, and then the leaves.
Nothing is lighter than a falling leaf.

Did the guns whisper when they spoke
That day? Did death tiptoe his business?
And afterwards in another world

Did mourners put on light mourning,
Casual as rain, as snow, as leaves?
Did a few tears fall?

Blood Stains

blood stains   how to remove   from cotton
silk   from all fine fabrics   blood stains
where did I read   all I remember old stains
harder than fresh   old stains often indelible

blood stains   what did it say   from glass
shattered   from metal   memorial marble
how to remove   a clean soft cloth   was it
and plenty of tepid water   also from paper

headlines   dispatches   communiqués   history
white leaves   green leaves   from grass growing
or dead   from trees   from flowers   from sky
from standing from running water   blood stains

Cromwell

After the celebrated carved misericords
And various tombs, the amiable sexton
Shows you by St. Mary's door the stone
Where Cromwell's men sharpened their swords.

Was it not a just, a righteous, war
When indiscriminate Irish blood
Flowed for the greater glory of God
Outside St. Mary's door?

If righteousness be often tipped with steel,
Be rightly tipped, psalm-singing men
Will help themselves to holy stone
To whet their zeal.

So you have both: the mellow misericords
Gracing the choir
And just outside the door
The swords.

City

In the scare
city
no scarcity
of fear
of fire
no scarcity
of goons
of guns
in the scare
city
the scar
city

A Fear

Against a falling snow
I heard him long ago

A young man who could prove
Old Goethe could not love

Old love he both denied
And equally decried.

If I were young and cold
I'd be afraid to scold

The old in love for fear
The god of love might hear

And hearing me might freeze
My five extremities.

Epitaphs

The Proud and Passionate Man

Stiff both in passion and in pride
He culminated when he died.

Fisherman

Now comes the fisherman to terms
Who erstwhile worked his will on worms.

The Furred Lady

What can this careful lady think
Who always wore in winter mink
Here on a day as cold as doom
To leave her mink wrap in her room?

Butcher

Falleth the rain, falleth the leaf,
The butcher now is one with beef.

Everyman

Preacher or lecher, saint or sot,
What he was once he now is not.

Undertaker

The man who yesterday was seen
On death to fatten on death grows lean.

Tomb of a Well-Known Soldier

Here lies the military mind,
Alas, not all of it there is,
Though while he lived he was inclined
To act as though it all were his.

Preacher

He called on God to smite the foe.
Missing his aim, God laid him low.

Old Lady Patriot

How calm she lies in death, how calm
This one-time champion of the Bomb.

Diplomat

Here lies a diplomat, alas,
Brought to one more complete impasse.

Going to the Funeral

Death hushes all   the bigwigs   the big shots
the top brass   the bashaws   the bullet-proof
bosses   the shoguns   in long black dreadnaughts
come purring   the magnates   shipping   oil
the magnificoes   Oh my God   the unimpeachables
the homburgs   the silk hats   the sucked cigars
death hushes   death hushes   the czars   the nabobs
and still they come purring   the moguls   the mugwumps
the high-muck-a-mucks   Oh my God   Oh my God!

Prescription

Whoever would be clean
Of cluttering desire
Must scrap the golden mean
And bed with frost or fire.

Only two ways to cure
The old itching disease:
No middle temperature
But only burn or freeze.

253

Water Poem

Waterflowers have no need to fear
The waterfowler since waterflowers
And fowlers live in different watery worlds.

Only waterfowl have a need to fear
The waterfowler whereas waterflowers
Only need to fear the fouling of waters.

Waterfowlers need a stamp to shoot
At waterfowl but waterflowers need
No stamp to shoot, no stamp at all at all.

Though a Fool

The wayfaring man though a fool
Will often fare as well
As one who has been to school
And knows how to scan and spell.

The scholar is melancholy
Too often on his way
While the fool may well be jolly
Though why he cannot say.

Exemplary

They never ask for more
Or ever lose their poise
Never a slammed door
Never a needless noise.

For slander a deaf ear
So faultlessly well bred
Gossip they seldom hear
The deferential dead.

Three Ships

Oh for three ships, three gallant ships
On Christmas day
And every day in the morning.

Not battleship   marksmanship   brinkmanship
On Christmas day
Or any day in the morning.

But kinship   friendship   fellowship
On Christmas day
And every day in the morning.

(Two Poems)

Stainless and steel
steeled against stain
where is the public man
year after year
unstainable
clean in his hardness
still public and still man?

Do not bend
do not bend the knee
to Baal
to Moloch
to the Pentagon
do not fold
do not fold the hands.

Suspension

Where bees bowing from flower to flower
In their deliberation
Pause

And then resume—wherever bees
Cruising from goldenrod
To rose

Prolong the noon the afternoon
Fanning with wings of spun
Bronze

Sweetness on the unruffled air
Calore and *colore*
Where bees

The Bells: Italy

What are they saying that must be said
over and over?

As if the hills could not be trusted
a silent language?

Why so great certainty age on age,
hour after hour?

Or is it a question they keep asking
no one can answer?

Bouquets

One flower at a time, please
however small the face.

Two flowers are one flower
too many, a distraction.

Three flowers in a vase begin
to be a little noisy

Like cocktail conversation,
everybody talking.

A crowd of flowers is a crowd
of flatterers (forgive me).

One flower at a time. I want
to hear what it is saying.

Chrysanthemums

Your opulence in the fading year
Your daring, coming so late, an almost
Winter flower.

Your name is gold but you yourself
Bronze rather or snow or lemon.
Still you are golden.

Fountain of petals caught unfalling
Why are you not offspring of August
Riches to riches?

Three Old Ladies and Three Spring Bulbs

I wouldn't be buried in anything but black
silk said Anne over her teacup
as the December afternoon dimmed to dusk.

I wouldn't be buried in anything but a white-
satin-and-ermine-lined incorruptible cypress
casket said Bertha over her stock quotations.

I would be buried in anything at all
said Clare at the open window my ashes
will sift as light as pear petals or snowflakes.

But Crocus, Hyacinth, and Tulip
brooding in autumn leaf-fall said I wouldn't
be buried in anything but good black earth.

Snowspell

Look, it is falling a little
faster than falling, hurrying
straight down on urgent business
for snowbirds, snowballs, glaciers.

It is covering up the afternoon.
It is bringing the evening down
on top of us and soon the night.
It is falling fast as rain.

It is bringing shadows wide
as eagles' wings and dark
as crows over our heads.
It is falling, falling fast.

Boy at a Certain Age

Perfectly rounded yet how slender
Supple, pliable, puppy-limber
Whole body lifts to lift a finger.

A mouth efficient for drinking, eating
Just as sufficient for shouting, beeping
But not yet for connected speaking.

A voice combining bass and treble
A mind more dreamable than thinkable
From chin to toe smooth as a pebble.

The Half Twist

What the camera did
To what the diver was doing

Alone by the lamp I
Contemplate I watch

What the camera did
To what the diver was doing

Not bird quite
And not quite human

What the camera did
To what the diver was doing.

The House Remembers

Faces, voices, yes of course
and the food eaten and the fires kindled
but the house also remembers feet.

Especially how one big pair used to pad
about comfortable as a cat's
bare on the bare wood floor.

And somebody else in clean white heavy socks
(his boots left at the door) would curl up
tailor-wise, Buddha-wise, on the couch

And only then the talk could really begin
and go on without end while listener
sat opposite and listened.

And once when one big toe had broken bounds
how someone took the sock and darned it
while the wearer sat and wondered.

Blisters to operate on but before
the sterile needle the basin of warm water
and someone kneeling as in the Last Supper.

What fireplace naturally remembers
are the cold feet it warmed but does it
recall the time when fire was not enough

And someone took bare feet in his bare hands
and chafed and cheered the blood
while the fire went on quietly burning?

When I Come

Once more the old year peters out—
all brightness is remembered
brightness.

> *(When I come, Bob,*
> *it won't·be while just on my way*
> *to going somewhere else.)*

A small pine bough with nothing
better to do fingers
a windowpane.

> *(When I come, Bob—)*

Against the wet black glass a single
oval leaf fixed
like a face.

His Running My Running

Mid-autumn late autumn
At dayfall in leaf-fall
A runner comes running.

How easy his striding
How light his footfall
His bare legs gleaming.

Alone he emerges
Emerges and passes
Alone, sufficient.

When autumn was early
Two runners came running
Striding together

Shoulder to shoulder
Pacing each other
A perfect pairing.

Out of leaves falling
Over leaves fallen
A runner comes running

Aware of no watcher
His loneness my loneness
His running my running.

Retrospect

Yes, I was one of them. And what a cast
Of characters we were, a medley, hodgepodge,
No two with the same tongue, same skin, same god.
You would have guessed a carnival was coming,
Itinerant bazaar. Bazaar? Bizarre!

And the gifts, those blessed gifts, the gold for instance,
What a fine sample of irrelevance!
For if the child had actually been royal
He would have had more gold already than all
Our camels could bear. But if he was in fact
What all the evidence of our eyes declared
He was, a peasant baby, why then our gold
Was for the first robber who came along.
Or barring that, say the poor father tried
To buy a blanket for the kid, a warm
Blanket, picture the shopkeeper and his sneer:
Aha! just how did you come into *this*?

As for the frankincense, it would have taken
More than a ton of it to quell the reek
In that cowbarn. Yet I must say the steaming
Dung (and watch your step) and the cows themselves
Their warm flanks, their inoffensive breath
Made that cold spot appreciably less chilly.

I said I was one of them. Let me take that back.
If I was one of them or one *with* them
In going, I wasn't when we left for home—
Our separate and strangely scattered homes.
They had more faith than I. That is the way
They saw it. I, I was less credulous.
They found what they set out to find, believed
What they were ready, were programmed, to believe.
Do I sound superior? I don't mean to be.
I know as well as the next man that faith,
Some measure of faith, is needed by us all.
Pure doubt is death.
                          It was a long journey,
Long both in going and long in the return.
Tell me, why do we travel? Is it to find
What no one anywhere will ever find?
Or is it rather to find what we could just
As well have found at home? Travel? Travail.

Of course, to say the child was not a prince
Is not to say he may not, somehow, sometime,
Rise from his class, conceivably become
A peasant leader, a rebel, yes, a name.
Such things are not unknown. Or let us say
Someday a poet. There have been instances.
Who knows? A holy man? Yes, even a prophet?

O no, I don't rule out the chance our journey
—In spite of all I've said—still may have been
A little better than mistaken.

1976

New Poems

"Love It from a Distance, Stella"

Something, I concede, can be said for distance
Though distance was never loved by love.

Art—the sculptured nude—is a different matter.
Whoever burned to possess cold marble?

Distance is something love diminishes.
Love waves a wand and distance disappears.

Still, something can be said for distance.
Possessor does not necessarily possess.

Love without distance—how easily love lost!
"Love it from a distance, Stella.

"Save your money, bargain or no bargain."
But what does Stella say? Ah, what does Stella?

"Oh, What Have I to Do with Time?"

Though Emerson may snub Time
Time will not snub Emerson.

Though Emerson may be deaf
To clocks, may disparage clocks

The clocks are ticking just
The same in Emerson's house.

Little clocks and grandfather clocks
Ticking ticking away for Emerson.

Though Emerson refuses to count
His hours beside the sea

267

This is not to say
The waves ever stop counting.

As for deadlines, however he
May defy or deny them

There is a certain deadline
In 1882 he can't deny.

Do I then disparage Emerson?
Oh no. For I myself

In growing old and ever
Older am disposed to give

The Universal Bully a cool
If not quite cold shoulder.

"Island Rejoices as Navy Departs"

salvos   explosions of laughter
healths   toasts   tossing of flowers
and everybody dancing down by the sea
The waves beside them danced but they
*Outdid the sparkling waves in glee.**

a rose in her hair   a rose behind his ear
and in the air everywhere roses
all the bells ringing   everybody singing
a jubilee   a jubilation   a jamboree
The waves beside them danced.

by night bonfires   beacons   searchlights
crisscrossing and kissing overhead
and high huge golden flowers of fire
shedding gold petals   even the dead
somehow are there   *The waves beside them.*

*Wordsworth

Blueberries

faint blue   dark blue   their bloom
untarnished   wild rose   ferns
the hayscented   brushing a granite boulder

blueberries   highbush   lowbush
and silence   old-fashioned silence
a single towee   "drink your teee"

white clouds   sky pasture   blueberries
a bird's booty   a boy's occupation
stain of blueberry on a boy's mouth

and all around the blueberry-colored
hills   dark blue   faint blue   blue
beyond blue   the farther the fainter

silence   except once and again
an invisible valley train like a
lost calf bawling-calling its mother

is it Butter Hill   or the northern Kearsarge
or the little hills of Concord and Henry
fresh out of jail   sun standing still

Sunday morning   gleam of white steeple
bell unheard   oh nothing heard at all
save solitary soliloquizing cricket

sweetfern   John Greenleaf   and juniper
the blueberry-pickers lost to one another
"the August day ablaze on lonely hills"

Ladybird, Ladybird
For Dorothy Donnelly

Wise one
having slept through the worst of winter
in some cool cranny
some secret esoteric crack
a snug bug if ever, you now emerge
in full sun
on the inner surface of my windowpane
thus wise again
for outside the glass there is still ice.

First harbinger
(or should I say pre-harbinger?) of spring
you come with something of the burst
of genie out of bottle
hitting in flight the glass
with almost inaudible tick,
ah, ladybird, ladybird beetle!

You pause
in momentary rest and I watch
till once more your burnt-sienna shell
parts and your gauze wings spread
so to repeat past performances
then for a jiffy scurry about
on invisible feet.

Come night
you are here again
arriving with a more plosive ping
on the parchment shade of my reading lamp
then flit to my page
to idle there like an animated
asterisk.

Light brings the summer midnight moth.
Is it light or warmth or both
brings you to luxuriate and expand
to adventure, yea, to voyage
under my electric sun?

What a tall tale
I could tell if I wanted to
for no one to believe: an angel
sent to cheer a lone man's evening chair
tiny enough to teach *multum in parvo*
not by speech but by dumb show.

Spell

To be near
Yet not to wake
The sleeper, to hear
The poised antiphony
Of breath taken,
Breath released, to see
The petal lips parted,
The fluid hair
Poured on the pillow
Like some rare metal
Curiously spun,
To be there,
Oh, to be there.

271

St. Brigid's

High
in the open arches
of St. Brigid's belltower

they sit
and contemplate
or if not contemplate

observe
the visible, only
the visible daylight world

the actual
undoctored unindoctrinated
world, the non-theological landscape.

Then
as the spirit moves
and only as the spirit moves

with merely
an initial flap of wings
unfold, detach themselves, take off

and thus
in arcs of perfect confidence
and no less perfect nonchalance descend

to tree
rooftree or grass or wheeling
reascend, float upward, and so gain

again
those welcoming arches
all twelve of them that lure them home.

Doves
who come and go to church
without ever going to church at all

bending
to their own dove devices
that massive immoveable institution.

Below
do the little priests
scheme to dislodge or utterly destroy them?

If so
priestcraft itself
is thwarted for the birds remain.

How
absolute, how beautiful
this dove indifference to Rome

to Brigid
herself whether the saint
or that earlier Irish mother goddess

of fire
fertility, agriculture
household arts and of course wisdom—

also
to mass, confession, Thursday
bingo and to the North Italian style.

Yes
indifferent even to time
and the belltower's hourly counting bell

and if
to time no less
indifferent to eternity.

Ah
serendipitous doves
who lacking wit have all the luck in the world.

If There Are Angels

If there are actually angels
As Arnold* says there are

I pray they bless me
Daily, nightly, with a little

Silence white like deep snow
Falling on a deserted street

After midnight, no sound except
The fitful stir of embers

On my hearth, my teakettle's
Soliloquy, and (if a dog

Must bark) a dog almost
Too distant to be heard.

If there actually are angels
May they bring me music

Too casual to be called
Music, too natural. For example

Surf-sounding wind in pines,
Tooting of a soft train,

Or Frost's canny bird singing
(But singing only a moment

For safety) in its sleep.
From archangels, Uriel, Gabriel, Michael

And all their peers I
Do not ask any attention.

To do so, what presumption!
Rather some lesser humbler angel

In the angelic hierarchy's lowest
Echelon. Or pair of angels

Who perhaps like Roman police
Fresh-groomed and white-gloved

Go about in cool, unobtrusive
Gentle, harmonious pairs. May they

Preserve me from all racket
Especially from all musical bellowing

Whether rock or grand opera,
Blessing me now and then

With some young velvet tenor
Whose voice simply floats upward.

If, as I say. If,
As Arnold says there are.

*See "The Disavowers of Angels"
  By the Reverend Arnold Kenseth.

Yes, What?

What would earth do without her blessed boobs
her blooming bumpkins garden variety
her oafs   her louts   her yodeling yokels
and all her Breughel characters
under the fat-faced moon?

Her nitwits   numskulls   universal
nincompoops   jawohl   jawohl   with all
their yawps   burps   beers   guffaws
her goofs   her goons   her big galoots
under the red-face moon?

Non Angli, Sed Angeli

Alastair, Cyril, Hilary, Ian, Ivor, Nigel, and Osbert
Have been to Oxford or if not to Oxford to Cambridge
Or if they haven't been will soon be going.

Fluently they finger flute, flageolet, or recorder
But their speaking voices are not indifferent music.

In a bookstore for instance one of them is inquiring:
"Do you happen to have *Italian without a Master*?"

Of course to those who know them nextdoor or nearer
Alastair, Cyril, Hilary, Ian, Ivor, Nigel, and Osbert
May shine, shall we say? a shade less than golden.

To David's Plants
(With a pitcher for their watering)

If David were Sultan you could be
His harem, why not? docile, spicy.
But since he isn't and you aren't
You're just a bunch of potted plants.

This pitcher to help quench your thirst.
I know your nicknames, have a typed list,
The whole thirteen. You don't know me?
Oh, just a friend of your friend D.

Poppycock

Could be a game
like battledore
and shuttlecock.
Could be.

Could be a color
red
but none of your Commy red
damn you!

Red of a cocky cock's
cockscomb
or scarlet poppies
popping in a field of wheat.

But poppycock
after all
alas is only
poppycock.

In other words bilge
bosh
buncombe
baloney

ballyhoo from Madison A
ballyhoo from Washington DC
red-white-and-blue poppycock.
Hurrah!

There are other cocks
to be sure.
Petcocks
weathercocks

barnyard cocks
bedroom cocks
cocksure
or cockunsure.

But to get back to poppycock
what a word!
God, what a word!
Just the word!

Keep your damn poems
only give me the words
they are made of.
Poppycock!

Monster

Less bird than bullet
its so-called wings
not wings at all.

And you? Don't say
you fly. You are
a piece of freight

packed in the bullet
shot through the air
how far from celestial!

And should it fail
it will not fall
like a broken bird

Icarus into the sea
Oh no   Oh no
but crash, burn, twist.

Morning Moon

Yo-ho, old Moon! Still up and shining?
You who while I lay snoozing-snoring
In crystal silence crossed the sky
And now look down on me in bed,
West-window Moon, with still
One winter hour to shine.

Full face, or some would say, fool face,
Fatuous yet somehow seeming wise
Like Shakespeare's fools, wise
With a half-wit wisdom all your own.

Soon when you fade and finally go
It will be just that. No ballyhoo.
No fanfare like the setting sun's.
Good morning, Moon, good bye.

Two Ghosts

Amherst. Dark hemlocks conspiring at the First Church
midway between the Mansion on Main Street and the
back entrance (the escape door) of the Lord Jeffery Inn.
Between one and two after midnight.

R Someone is here. Angelic? Or demonic?
E Someone less than someone.
R Emily?
E How could you divine me?
R An easy guess, you who were ghost while living
   and haunting us ever since.
E A ghost to catch a ghost?
R A poet to catch a poet.
E And you—you must be the Robert who said:
   "The petal of the rose it was that stung."
   Or did *I* say it?
R We both have said it now.
E Sweet the bee—but rose is sweeter—
   Quick his sting—but rose stings deeper—
   Bee will heal—rose petal—never
R You talk of bees who were yourself white moth.
E Seldom flitting so far from home.
   Oftener the other way to touch my stone.
   Have you seen it?
R *Called Back*?
E The stone keeps calling me back.
R I would have cut a different epitaph.
   Called on. Called ahead.
E But on and back are both one now, aren't they?
R My stone is not a stone but a heap, a pile—
E Why should immortality be so stony?
R —a mass, a mausoleum, a mock mountain
   over there. Have you seen?
E Oh, I took *that* for a factory or fort.
R Fort of learning, factory of scholars.
   And my name cut deep in granite. Have you seen?
E I never dared to go so far—so near.
R "Less than someone," you said. I say,
   "More than someone." You are a name now, Emily.
E Why do they hunt me so?
R The scholar-scavengers?

279

E   Once I could hide but now
they try my mind, they pry
apart my heart.

R   We were both hiders. You
in your father's house. I
in the big buzzing world.
I craved to be understood
but feared being wholly known.

E   You said, "Anything more than the truth
would have seemed too weak."

R   And you, "Truth like ancestors' brocades
can stand alone." I should say truth
is not the dress but the naked lady.

E   Or naked gentleman.

R   Have it as you will.

(A tower clock strikes two)

R   There's truth for you.
To tell the truth
Is all a clock can do.

E   But clocks are human—like us all—
They err—grow ill—and finally fail.

R   They never lie intentionally.

E   Why did you say, "Nature's first green is gold?"
Some buds, yes, but the buds of beech are cinnamon,
and the swamp maple—but need I tell you?

R   And why—why did you say:
"Nature rarer uses yellow than another hue?"
Think of the dandelions, Emily, the fields
of solid yellow. Think of the forsythias
and buttercups. The sugar maple's pendant blooms,
the cowslips, cinquefoil, golden Alexanders,
the marigolds and all the goldenrods.
Witch-hazel and October trees: beech, elm,
maple, popple, apple!

E   Why did Emerson, your Emerson, my Emerson, say,
"Succory to match the sky?" Imagine!

R   Your lines that haunt me most—

E   What are they?

R   "After great pain a formal feeling comes.
The nerves sit ceremonious like tombs."

E   Oh! Oh!

R   "After great pain—"

E   And that line of yours:
    "Weep for what little things could make them glad."
R   I was writing of children.
E   We are all children.
R   Laugh at what little things could make them weep.
E   Can make us all weep. Were you a believer?
R   I took the dare to believe. I made myself
    believe I believed. And you?
E   Two angels strove like wrestlers in my mind:
    one belief, one disbelief.
R   "After great pain—"
E   Oh!
R   Emily? Emily!

D

Deliberate
Determined
Undeterred

The cliffs stand out against the sea
Cliff beyond cliff, each cliff a D.

The sea assaults them as the sea will;
The cliffs still stand there, stand there still

Dauntless
Defiant
Undismayed.

                Ah, but sometimes the sea
                Forgets ferocity
                And like a purring cat
                Curls at their feet.

Gulls Resting

Those enviable gulls whose art
it is to rest
whenever they choose to rest
in any of three elements:
now bobbing on waves like sitting ducks,
now roosting pigeon-wise along some seaside roof,
and now aloft
moving and still moving with unmoved wings
at rest in air on air.

Automatons
their freedom in flight is no less faultless
and though their form
form of the flying flock
is only the pattern of tossed dice
still it is all we ask.
Scavengers, still how they transmute, transcend
—those curving throats—those breasts—
to absolute snow!

Pedal Point

After snow-silence now once more
The faint fanged roar
Of thunder.

      Time is on the sly and I am slowly dying.

Listen! Wild geese, their aerial wedge
Like an old motion picture flickers
And fades.

      Time is on the sly and I am slowly dying.

Out of May mist the toads
Like birds trilling
Their nuptials.

But soon, singly, the leaves
Or a windy scattering
Of leaves.

Now katydid slows his fiddling,
Slows and ceases. Day dream,
Deep dream.

Night and a young poet walking
The unlit darkness knocks
On my door.

    Time is on the sly and I am slowly dying.

Fire Chaconne

1
Flare of match
Cupped hands its vestal temple.

2
Firefly, your green
Spark on the green darkness.

3
I burn
Therefore I am.

4
Single in window
Candle, what are you saying?

5
What fate?
Wind or your own down-burning?

6
The cold stars
Their incredible heat.

7

Blue juniper
Berry: two summers' sun.

8

Con fuoco
You violins, your incandescence.

9

Flaming in fall
Gorgeous the poison ivy.

10

"Scotland's burning.
Pour on water." No, no, not Scotland.

11

Ambivalent fire
Our love, our life, our fear.

12

Scarlet the night sky.
Bonfire, beacon, holocaust?

13

"God is love.
Reader, flee from the wrath to come."

14

Savonarola
The stones of Florence still weeping.

15

Fire lizard?
How far the moist woodland salamander!

16

The salt sea
Dyes the driftwood hearth.

17

True poem
Burns with undiminishing fuel.

18
Bonfire on snow
Twice beautiful: symbol and fact.

19
Almighty sun
Father of all our fires.

20
Fire opal
As if all gems were flashing.

Library of Congress Cataloging in Publication Data
Francis, Robert, 1901–
  Collected poems, 1936–1976.
PS3511.R237A6   1976   811'.5'2   76-8753
ISBN 0-87023-211-8